YESTERDAY'S KITCHEN

YESTERDAY'S KITCHEN

Jewish communities and their
food before 1939

Compiled and edited by

GILLIAN BURR with
MARION COHEN

A helpful '8' book

VALLENTINE MITCHELL

First published in 1993 in Great Britain by
VALLENTINE MITCHELL & CO LTD.
Gainsborough House, Gainsborough Road,
London E11 1RS, England

and in the United States of America by
VALLENTINE MITCHELL
c/o International Specialized Book Services, Inc.
5804 N.E. Hassalo Street, Portland, OR 97213-3644

British Library Cataloguing in Publication Data

Yesterday's Kitchen: Jewish Communities and
    Their Food Before 1939.
    I. Burr, Gillian II. Cohen, Marion
    641.5

ISBN 0 85303 264 5

Library of Congress Cataloging-in-Publication Data

Burr, Gillian.
Yesterday's kitchen: Jewish communities and their food
    before 1939/compiled and edited by Gillian Burr
    with Marion Cohen.
        p.   cm.
    "A helpful '8' book."
    Includes index.
    ISBN 0–85303–264–5
    1. Cookery, Jewish. 2. Cookery, International. 3. Jews–
        History–70-1789–Outlines, syllabi, etc. 4. Jews–History–1789-1945–
        Outlines, syllabi, etc. I. Cohen, Marion.
    II. Title.
    TX724.B866   1993   93–30054
    641.5'676–dc20   CIP

Typeset by Regent Typesetting, London
Printed in Great Britain by BPCC Wheatons Ltd, Exeter

This book is dedicated to the memory of the Jewish victims of persecution who did not survive and to the courage of those who did.

Contents

Acknowledgements

We should like to thank all the contributors who have shared their memories and recipes with us.

The following individuals and organisations have given us invaluable help with research and advice:

Christa Wichman and the Trustees of the Weiner Library;
London Museum of Jewish Life;
University of London Library, Senate House;
Mr Naim Dangoor, Editor of *The Scribe* magazine;
Mavis Hyman, author of *Indian-Jewish Cooking*;
Vera Grodzinski;
the Embassies of Denmark, Israel and Morocco and the Jamaican High Commission.

Our grateful thanks also go to all those who have helped, in practical ways, to put this book together:

Joan Stiebel, Ruth Smilg, David, Gordon and Rosanna Burr, Carole Chesterman, Anita Faith, Barbara Green, Caroline and Nicholas Posnansky, Ruth Starr, Lorraine Young.

All statistics are from the Institute of Jewish Affairs and the relevant Jewish Year Books.

Picture credits

Photographs on pages 7, 12, 13 (top) and 29 are from the London Museum of Jewish Life; those on pages 11 and 13 (bottom) are from Bildarchiv, Abraham Pisarek.

Introduction

This book was commissioned to commemorate the sixtieth anniversary of the founding of the Central British Fund for World Jewish Relief which was initially formed to rescue Jews from Nazi Europe. It was, therefore, originally intended to reflect the cooking in the communities affected by Nazi persecution. However, since the Second World War C.B.F. has helped Jews escape from persecution in other countries, particularly Arab lands and Eastern Europe. We therefore decided to broaden the boundaries of the book and include food from Jewish communities around the world.

Yesterday's Kitchen is very much a collection of personal memories of the cooking of the time, and of the occasions on which it was traditionally served. We have included basic outlines of the histories of the Jewish communities of some thirty-nine different countries from all five continents.

The recipes have been contributed by people whose families originated in different places and who came from varied backgrounds. The spellings of the names of foreign foods and recipes have not been standardised. We have given them here as they have been given to us; hence halva/halwa, hameem/hamin. We hope that this book will help to preserve the individual recipes and styles of cooking which are part of the Jewish heritage and which are in danger of being lost for ever.

All royalties from *Yesterday's Kitchen* will go to the Central British Fund for World Jewish Relief.

GILIAN BURR
MARION COHEN
London, 1993

MAPS AND HISTORIES
Western Europe

Western Europe, 1933

BELGIUM

Jewish population: 1933, *60,000*
1992, *30,000*

It is known that Jews were living in Belgium in Roman times. They were expelled or massacred during the Great Plague in 1348. There was an influx of Marranos in the early sixteenth century following the Spanish Inquisition; the Ashkenazim came into Belgium during the eighteenth century while Belgium was under Austrian rule. In 1830, when Belgium became independent, the status of Jews was formally recognised and full freedom of religion was granted a year later.

By 1940, the population had increased to approximately 100,000, of whom 20,000 were refugees from Germany. During the war, 25,000 Jews were hidden by Belgians and thus saved.

The community today is primarily Ashkenazi with small Sephardi communities in Antwerp and Brussels. As in all countries, the immigrants continued to cook their traditional foods in their new homeland and a typical Friday night meal would reflect the family's origin: gefilte fish balls, chicken soup with kneidlach, braised chicken, carrot tzimmes, potato chremslech (page 154) and braised chicory, which was particularly popular. This would have been followed by honey cake and a compote consisting of stewed apple, poached sliced pears and poached prunes.

DENMARK

Jewish population: 1933, *6,000*
1992, *9,000*

Jews first settled in Denmark by invitation during the early seventeenth century. Sephardi Jews were allowed to settle anywhere in the country, but Ashkenazi Jews needed special dispensation. Civic equality was granted in 1814 and political equality in 1849.

The population was increased at the beginning of the twentieth century with Russian Jews fleeing the pogroms. At the outbreak of the Second World War there were 7,500 Jews in Denmark. After the German occupation of Denmark, the agreement by the Danes to protect their Jewish community was broken. A magnificent rescue operation was put into effect and all but 472 Jews were smuggled out to safety in Sweden. Those remaining were deported to Theresienstadt, where forty-nine perished.

In 1969, 2,500 Polish Jewish refugees settled in Denmark. Nearly all Danish Jews live in Copenhagen and the community is almost wholly Ashkenazi. Denmark supplies kosher meat to Norway where Shechita is not permitted.

The foods available in Denmark are similar to those in Britain, with great emphasis on dairy products. Denmark supplies kosher butter, cheese and eggs to Britain. Jewish cooking in Denmark is Ashkenazi and the traditional Friday night meal would have been chopped liver, chicken soup, chicken and vegetables. Alternatively, in summer, a fish meal would be served and rødgrød (page 179) with cream for dessert.

FRANCE

Jewish population: 1933,   *280,000*
1992,   *600,000*

The first Jews in France came with the Greeks in about 500 BCE and new communities were established after the destruction of the Second Temple. In 1306 CE Jews were expelled from France and took refuge in Alsace, which at that time was part of the German Holy Roman Empire, although some remained in communities in southern France. Alsace became part of France in 1648.

After the French Revolution, Jews were granted equal rights and with Napoleon's help a Sanhedrin was established in 1807. In 1831 the Jewish religion was recognised as one of the three religions supported by the State. Despite anti-semitism, individual Jews played an increasingly prominent role in French life during the second half of the nineteenth century and attained wealth and position.

The community was increased by a wave of immigrants from Eastern Europe at the turn of this century and further increased by German Jews fleeing Nazi persecution in the 1930s. During the Second World War about 120,000 Jews were deported or killed, but with the influx of Jews from Eastern Europe, North Africa and Egypt after the war, the numbers of French Jewry have increased to about 600,000. This number includes the long-established Alsace community of orthodox Ashkenazi Jews, families of Eastern European descent and Sephardi Jews from Egypt and North Africa who make up half the total community.

The traditional cooking among French Jews before the war was therefore mainly Ashkenazi, although among the well-established, wealthy French Jews the influence of French *haute cuisine* was paramount. There is a strong belief among French Jews that pâté de foie gras was adapted by the French from Jewish chopped liver. The traditional Friday night dinner would have been chicken soup (page 85), roast chicken or goose, followed by a fruit tart.

HOLLAND

Jewish population: 1933, *157,000*
     1992, *25,000*

The small medieval Jewish community was virtually wiped out by persecutions at the time of the Black Death. The present community dates from the end of the sixteenth century when Marranos from Antwerp and other Sephardi Jews from Portugal, Italy and Turkey make their home in Holland. Ashkenazi Jews came from Poland, Lithuania and Germany in the early seventeenth century when there was freedom to worship. Since 1792 Jews have had the same constitutional rights as all other citizens and since 1797 Jews have been admitted to Parliament.

During the seventeenth and eighteenth centuries Jews played an active part in the flourishing commercial and intellectual life of Holland. Before the onset of the Second World War the number of Dutch Jews had already begun to decline, but even so some 100,000 perished at the hands of the Nazis. Today, more than 90 per cent of Dutch Jews are Ashkenazi, most of whom are middle-class professionals.

The cookery of Dutch Jews is mainly of Ashkenazi influence, despite the community's origins being Sephardic. Meat features quite dominantly in main courses and, in common with most communities where many were poor, all permitted parts of the animal were used. Hence the inclusion here of stuffed spleen or miltz (page 111), and elsewhere in this book fried brains croquettes (page 115), perrogen (page 70) which uses both spleen and lungs, braised sweetbreads (page 117) and the various recipes for calf's foot. The rich dairy pastures of Holland were reflected in much Dutch Jewish baking, with buttery cakes and biscuits being extremely popular.

ITALY

Jewish population: 1933, *47,500*
     1992, *35,000*

A Jewish community existed in Italy in the second century BCE and until the fourth century CE when Christianity was made the official religion of the Roman Empire and the persecution of Jews began. In the Middle Ages, Jews living in Rome, southern Italy and parts of northern Italy flourished in relatively peaceful circumstances and founded centres of learning. The community was increased by refugees from Spain and Germany. In 1555 Pope Paul IV issued a Bill condemning Jews to live in separate areas – ghettos – and limiting their choice of work. The ghettos continued to exist until after the French Revolution when they were abolished and the Jews were emancipated. They were granted equal rights in 1870 on the unification of Italy. During the early years of Fascism (1922–38) Italian Jews were not persecuted. This altered with the introduction, under Nazi pressure, of the racial laws, although Jews were not deported until after the German occupation in 1943. Nearly 8,500 Jews were deported to Auschwitz, of whom only 511 survived. The community today is mainly Sephardi, with immigrants from Egypt (1956) and Libya (1967).

As Italy has always been markedly regional, the cooking of the Jewish communities varied from region to region (there are at least four different versions of charoseth in Mira Sacerdoti's *Italian Jewish Cooking*). Some influences in Italian Jewish cooking probably date back as far as Roman times, but others almost certainly include the Greeks (who came to Italy in the fifteenth century) and the Sephardim.

A typical Sabbath menu would often include a rice dish, followed by veal (pages 115–17) or poultry, with an almond or other rich cake for dessert. The Yom Kippur fast was broken with cake.

PORTUGAL

Jewish population: 1933,   *1,200*
                   1992,   *300*

Jews lived peacefully in Portugal until the Civil War in 1373 when the Jewish quarter of Lisbon was destroyed. In 1492 the Inquisition forced many to flee from Spain to Portugal where, in 1496, an order expelling Jews was repealed and they were forcibly baptised. These converts were known as Marranos. During the Napoleonic era a new community was established in Lisbon by British Jews from Gibraltar, and a certain amount of movement between the two countries continued well into this century. Just before the Second World War 70,000 refugees escaping Nazi persecution took refuge in Portugal *en route* to America, and some remained. By the end of the war the community numbered around 1,000.

The Jewish community in Portugal before the war was almost entirely Sephardi. From the host community they took the love of very sweet things like the Queijinhos (page 216). As in many Sephardi communities dfeena (page 105) was the common Shabbat lunch, although often in the heat of the summer cold chicken would be served with salads. Chicken or fried fish were the traditional Friday night dishes. For the Seder meal, vegetable soup was more commonly served than chicken soup and a popular dish for Passover, both here and in Spain, was bunuelos, fried potato balls served with a sugar syrup.

SPAIN

Jewish population: 1933,   *4,000*
                      1992,   *12,000*

Jews have been in Spain since Roman times and many of the early settlers were farmers or landowners, living in comparative freedom until the sixth century when anti-Jewish measures commenced. In the seventh century the Visigoths reduced the Jews to slavery. After the conquest of Spain by the Arabs in the eighth century, Jews regained the freedom to practise their religion, but were not given equal rights. Although there were persecutions at intervals, Jews flourished and many rose to great prominence in medicine, the arts and scholarship during medieval times – often known as the Golden Age in Spain.

In 1136 after the Almohad invasion, the practice of Judaism was forbidden and Maimonides had to flee persecution by the Almohads in 1148. The expanding Christianisation of the north of Spain actually offered easier conditions and there the Jews flourished, with considerable intellectual achievement. In 1391 persecution and massacres began, culminating in the Inquisition and the expulsion of the Jews in 1492 – 50,000 actually fleeing Spain. The Inquisition did not formally stop until 1834, and Marranos (converted Jews) were hounded throughout that time.

Jews began to drift back to Spain after 1869 when non-Catholics were granted rights of residence and religious practice. Before and during the Second World War many Jewish refugees were given safe passage through Spain, and Spanish officials helped rescue Jews in Hungary. The Madrid community was legally recognised in 1965 and the community is overwhelmingly Sephardi.

SWITZERLAND

Jewish population: 1933,   *17,970*
                      1992,   *19,000*

Jews first settled in Switzerland in the thirteenth century, but suffered persecutions and expulsions in the fourteenth century when they were blamed for the spread of the plague and the community was almost exterminated. In 1798, after the establishment of the Helvetian Republic, Jews were given freedom of movement, trade and residence, and they attained full civic rights in 1866. The first World Zionist Congress was held in Basle in 1897. During the Second World War, Switzerland sheltered 23,000 Jews, although it refused admission to at least 10,000 more.

The majority of Swiss Jews are Ashkenazi although there has been a small immigration of Sephardi Jews from Arab countries. There are about 25 communities, over half of which are German speaking and the largest of which are in Zurich, Geneva and Basle. Shechita is forbidden and kosher meat has to be imported.

Polly Solomons in her kitchen, England, 1936 (from Mr Bernard Salmon).

UNITED KINGDOM

Jewish population: 1933,   *300,000*
                1992,   *330,000* approx.

The first known Jewish settlements in England were after the Norman Conquest of 1066. They were mainly in London, Lincoln and York. There were massacres of Jews in 1190 and the entire York community was wiped out. Edward I expelled the Jews from England in 1290 and they were only re-admitted in 1655, by Oliver Cromwell, when the Spanish and Portuguese congregation in London was established. The Ashkenazi community became established at the end of the seventeenth century. A Bill for the political emancipation of the Jews was first passed in 1830 but it was not until 1858 that Lionel de Rothschild was sworn in as the first Jewish Member of Parliament. The Jewish communities flourished and many communal organisations were started. Between 1881 and 1914 there was a large influx of refugees from the Russian Empire. The population expanded from 25,000 in the 1850s to nearly 350,000 by 1914, although some refugees eventually continued their passage to North America or South Africa.

When the Nazis came to power in Germany in 1933 there was a further wave of Jewish immigration to England and a smaller influx occurred after 1956 from Arab countries and Eastern Europe. Britain has the distinction of being one of the few countries of Europe where during the last 300 years there have been no serious outbreaks of violence against Jews and a ghetto system has never been implemented.

The immigrants from Poland and Russia have had the greatest influence on British Jewish cooking and before the last war these immigrant communities produced meals as similar as possible to those in 'the Heim': borscht, herring, chulent, etc. As early as 1916, however, the cookery book *Dainty Dinners and Dishes for Jewish Families* contained recipes reflecting English cooking rather than Jewish (see plum cake (page 208) and Beaconsfield pudding (page 168)).

Among traditional families, Friday night dinner consisted of chopped liver, chicken soup, roast chicken with stuffing and, usually, a fruit pie. Among the poorer communities, a traditional Friday night main course was cold fried fish and gefilte fish balls, boiled and/or fried (fried gefilte fish seems to be unique to the United Kingdom).

Central Europe

GERMANY

Berlin

Cologne

Leipzig

Frankfurt

Breslau

Prague

CZECHOSLOVAKIA

Brno

Munich

Bratislava

Kosice

Mukachevo

Salzburg

Vienna

Debrecen

Czernowitz

AUSTRIA

Budapest

Iasi

HUNGARY

Kishinev

ROMANIA

Bucharest

Central Europe, 1933

AUSTRIA

Jewish population: 1933, *250,000*
1992, *10,000*

The first reference to Jews in Austria was in 906 CE. In the thirteenth and fourteenth centuries Vienna had one of the largest Jewish communities in Europe, but Jews became the victims of intense persecution during the ensuing centuries. Many were expelled or converted and although small numbers of Jews returned, they were all expelled in 1670. They again returned in small numbers and in 1782 the Edict of Toleration was issued. In 1867 Jews were given full rights, in keeping with many other European countries, although this did not indicate diminishing anti-semitism.

The twentieth-century Austrian Jewish community formed a highly educated and cultured society, numbering among its members Gustav Mahler, Sigmund Freud, Arnold Schönberg, Stephan Zweig and Theodore Herzl. Their influence on Western civilisation was immense. After the Anschluss on 13 March 1938, all Jewish activities were forbidden. During the next two years, however, approximately 120,000 Jews managed to escape. During the Second World War about 65,000 Austrian Jews were killed. Out of the 10,000 Jews now living in Austria, 20 per cent had their roots in Austria before 1938. Over half the population is aged over 60. The community is largely Ashkenazi and the majority of Jews live in Vienna, although there are provincial centres such as Baden and Salzburg.

Many of the Austrian recipes bear similarities to those from other countries in Central and Eastern Europe, as the foods at their disposal tended to be the same. Variations depended mainly on family traditions. A typical Friday evening meal would consist of stuffed carp (page 95), chicken soup, roast chicken or pot roast, dumplings, stewed fruit or pancakes (page 177).

CZECHOSLOVAKIA

Jewish population: 1933, *356,700*
1992, *12,000*

There is evidence to show that Jews lived in the area of Moravia in the ninth century and in Bohemia in the tenth century in relative peace and prosperity. Persecution of Jews began in earnest in 1096 when, during the First Crusade, many of the community were forced into baptism. After this, Jews were expelled at regular intervals but resettled when permission was granted. By the end of the sixteenth century there was an important Jewish community in Prague. In 1867, after continuing expulsions and prohibitions, including one on the number of Jewish families allowed to marry, Jews

A family in East Slovakia, 1930 (from Dr Ruth Gross).

received legal emancipation. They became increasingly assimilated into the general community.

Over the centuries, Prague has been regarded as the crown of European Jewry, containing one of the oldest synagogues in Europe – the Alt-Neu Schul – whose foundation dates back to the fourteenth century. After the fall of the Austro-Hungarian Empire in 1919, the newly independent Czech Republic recognised Jewish nationality and by 1935 the community numbered almost 357,000. Nazi Germany invaded in 1939 and those Jews who had not escaped were sent to Theresienstadt. At the end of the war there were only 42,000 Jews left in Czechoslovakia. Although Jews were prominent in the Communist government after the war, as a result of anti-semitism in 1952 many Jews emigrated and many more again after the Soviet invasion in 1968.

The present Jewish community is entirely Ashkenazi and is composed of survivors and people who returned after the war. They have equal rights of citizenship. Since the 1989 revolution, many Jews have become more overt about their religious origins and have been trying to revive the community.

Many of the Czechoslovakian Jewish recipes were indistinguishable from those of Austria and Hungary. Traditional Ashkenazi dishes for Shabbat predominated – chicken soup with farfel (page 78), chulent with kugel (page 104) and fruit compote.

GERMANY

Jewish population: 1933,   *510,000*
1992,   *40,000*

The history of the Jews in Germany goes back at least as far as the fourth century CE. Jewish settlements were encouraged in the eighth and ninth centuries and continued to flourish, particularly along the Rhine, one important centre being at Worms. The next few centuries saw major persecutions and expulsions and many Jews fled to Eastern Europe where the German dialect gradually developed into Yiddish. The situation for Jews in Germany began to improve in the seventeenth century after the Thirty Years War. With the French occupation of parts of Germany in the nineteenth century, Jews were emancipated and complete emancipation had been achieved by 1869 – which was ratified in the 1871 constitution – although there was discrimination in certain areas (the army, academia and the diplomatic corps). However, this period saw an incredible flourishing of intellectual, scientific and artistic life among the Jews in Germany, contributing elements of lasting value to civilisation. Yiddish was replaced by German and much of the community became assimilated.

Yom Tov table, Germany, 1938 (from Rabbi David Hulbert).

Couple seated at table, Germany, 1938 (from Rabbi David Hulbert).

Seder night, Berlin, 1937 (from Dr Ruth Gross).

From 1933, when the Nazis came to power, the community was gradually excluded from German life and in September 1935 the Nuremberg Laws were passed, the first of the major discriminatory laws against the Jews. These were followed by other decrees, essentially removing Jews from the protection of German law. Between 1933 and 1938 about half of the community fled abroad, mainly to the US, Britain, Argentina and Palestine. Deportations began in 1941 and about 180,000 German Jews died during the war. The number of Jews who remained in Germany in hiding during the war is estimated at 19,000.

After the war, many of the survivors emigrated to Israel. West Germany paid compensation to Jews for the consequences of the wartime persecutions, although this was not the case in East Germany (there has been an attempt to remedy this now). A slow trickle of Jews returned to settle in Germany and they were joined by refugees from Eastern Europe and, recently, from countries that made up the USSR. The community today is almost wholly Ashkenazi, although very few are the descendants of the original German Jews.

German Jewish recipes epitomise Ashkenazi cooking, with many warming, rich dishes. A characteristic dish is sweet/sour fish or meat (sauerbraten, pages 109–10). Tzimmes, for example, is a sweetened meat and vegetable dish which varies from country to country in Central and Eastern Europe. For instance, in Germany prunes were used (page 156), in Poland and Russia carrots were dominant, in Romania pumpkin and chickpeas, and in Hungary it was chestnuts (page 160).

In Germany the most popular dishes for a Shabbat meal were chicken soup with fine noodles, boiled tongue or roast chicken, potato salad (page 163) or red cabbage (page 148), and fruit compote (page 170) and apple cake (page 193).

HUNGARY

Jewish population: 1933, *444,500*
1940, *800,000*
1992, *85,000*

There were Jews in Hungary in Roman times; the earliest graves date from the second century CE. Jews were persecuted during early Magyar times, were expelled in 1349 and were allowed to return in 1364. Under Ottoman rule, Sephardi Jewish communities were established during the sixteenth and seventeenth centuries and were joined during the eighteenth century by Jews from Moravia and Bohemia. Learned orthodox Jews from Poland established yeshivot in the nineteenth and early twentieth centuries. Jews were emancipated in 1867. The history of Hungarian Jewry is similar to that of other European countries – a series of invitations to settle, followed by repetitive expulsions. Jews were finally given legal emancipation in 1867, despite increasing anti-semitism.

The number of Jews in Hungary was swollen between the First and Second World

Wars as Hungary annexed Slovakia, Carpatho-Ruthenia and Transylvania, each of these areas having old and important Jewish communities. Despite Hungary's alliance with Nazi Germany, and although Jews were recruited for labour under harsh military command, the Hungarian government refused to deport Hungarian Jews. This changed on 14 March 1944 when Germany occupied Hungary. About 600,000 Hungarian Jews, some three-quarters of Hungarian Jewry, were annihilated in the last nine months of the Second World War.

At present, the majority of Hungarian Jews are Ashkenazi and live in Budapest, but there are 23 provincial communities. Since the collapse of the Communist regime, there appears to be a revival of Hungarian Jewish life.

The main influences on Hungarian Jewish food were Ashkenazi, although the community adopted many elements of the host country, particularly the use of pepper, paprika, chestnuts and the popular goulash (served without the sour cream, of course (page 106)). Goose, roasted or casseroled was often served and many dishes used goose fat rather than chicken fat. A typical Friday night menu might be stuffed carp or pike (page 100), chicken soup with hand-made lokshen, boiled or stewed chicken with farfel and tzimmes, apple compote or strudel.

ROMANIA

Jewish population: 1933, *984,200*
1992, *23,000*

Jews have lived in the area of what is now Romania since Roman times. In 1367 there was an influx of refugees from Hungary, Sephardi refugees came in the sixteenth century, and in the seventeenth century Jews fleeing massacres in Poland and the Ukraine settled in Moldavia where they were warmly welcomed. Moldavia's rulers issued charters to attract Jews from surrounding countries and this contributed to the growth of the Jewish community. During the eighteenth and nineteenth centuries, as a result of wars between the Russian and Turkish empires, many more Jews took refuge in Moldavia. From 1826 to 1916 conditions deteriorated, with at least 200 regulations restricting the community's freedom, and 70,000 Jews emigrated. Equal rights were finally granted in 1919 although the disciminatory attitude continued. At the end of the First World War, Transylvania with its large Hungarian Jewish population became part of Romania.

In 1937 discriminatory legislation was introduced and Jews lost all rights of citizenship and were not permitted to practise in the professions. Romania allied itself to Germany at the beginning of the war, and in 1940 the large Chassidic community suffered particularly from the Nuremberg Laws; there were several massacres within Romania itself. Approximately 385,000 Romanian Jews were killed in the Second

World War, either by the Romanian armies, who collaborated vigorously with the Germans, or after deportation to extermination camps.

When Communist rule was established in 1946 a Jewish Democratic Committee was formed which was responsible for expelling and imprisoning Zionist supporters. Some 125,000 Jews emigrated to Israel in the years immediately after the establishment of the State and, since the 1960s, emigration to Israel has continued. At present the community is mainly Ashkenazi, half of which live in Bucharest with some 50 smaller communities and congregations scattered throughout the country.

Although the cooking was mainly Ashkenazi (often reflecting the traditions of the Polish and Hungarian immigrants), Turkish influences can be seen – for example, in the use of vine leaves (page 122) and aubergines (page 72). Along with many Central and Eastern European countries, there was a dearth of fresh vegetables during winter months and great use was made of pickled tomatoes, cucumbers, cabbage and even water melon.

Eastern Europe

Leningrad

LATVIA

Riga

LITHUANIA

Kovno ● Vilna

Moscow ●

SOVIET UNION

Warsaw
●

POLAND

● Lodz

Kiev ●

Lvov
●

Odessa
●

Eastern Europe, 1933

LATVIA

Jewish population: 1933, *96,300*
1992, *22,000*

The country of Latvia was formed by the territories of Livonia and Courland and there is evidence of Jews living in Riga – capital of the region – in 1536. When the area became part of the Russian Empire in the eighteenth century, those Jews who could prove that they had lived there for some time were allowed to remain; others were resettled in the Pale of Settlement. By 1897 three-quarters of the 26,793 Jews of Livonia lived in Riga. The Jews of Courland numbered about 51,000 and were influenced more by German culture than by Russian. Before the First World War there were about 190,000 Jews in the Latvian territories but many were expelled to the Russian interior during the war years.

The independent Latvian Republic was established in 1918. At first, a liberal spirit towards Jews flourished – by 1933 there were 98 Jewish elementary schools – but Fascism gradually developed and Latvia became a totalitarian state in 1934. In 1940, Latvia became part of the Soviet Union and just before the Nazis' attack on Latvia in 1941, the Soviet authorities deported thousands of Latvian Jews to Siberia and many more fled to the Russian interior. However, despite this, 75,000 fell to the Nazis. After the war a steady trickle of the Jews who had escaped into Russia returned to Latvia and by 1970 the Jewish population was estimated at nearly 50,000. Riga became one of the leading centres of political agitation among Jews in the Soviet Union.

The cooking in the Jewish community of Latvia was influenced by both Russian and German Ashkenazi cookery. Because of its similar geographical location, the food available to Latvian Jews differs little from that of Lithuanian Jews: plentiful fish – especially herring and mackerel; vegetables such as beetroot, cabbage and cucumbers, which would be pickled to last through the winter – for example, beetroot jam (page 213); fruits, particularly the berries, were only available in season and many of these would be preserved. Dairy products were important and buttermilk was a popular drink.

LITHUANIA

Jewish population: 1933, *155,125*
1992, *5,000*

A large and well-established Jewish community lived in historial Lithuania. Until the sixteenth century the community was on the fringes of European Jewry, but during the sixteenth and seventeenth centuries the influence of Polish Jewry was strong and their mode of learning and organisational methods were adopted in Lithuania. The community was relatively secure and free from persecution and there was a flourishing of religious life and learning in Lithuania, the most important leader and scholar being the Gaon of Vilna in the eighteenth century. The Jews of Lithuania maintained their own way of life, speaking a special dialect of Yiddish and having a reputation for intellectual rigour in their Torah learning.

By the end of the nineteenth century, over one and a half million Jews lived in the region (an eighth of the population), but at the end of the First World War the country was divided between Poland and the USSR, with Vilna and the majority of Jews coming under Polish rule, and the northern area becoming independent Lithuania. After independence, the Jews were given national and cultural rights and the government included a Minister for Jewish Affairs. However, in 1926 there was a right-wing revolution and the rapid growth of anti-semitism followed, including restrictions on employment and occupations. Between 1941 and 1944 the entire country was occupied by Germany. Most of the provincial communities were totally destroyed that first year, and by the end of the war 90 per cent of Lithuanian Jews had been exterminated.

Lithuanian Jewish cooking was wholly Ashkenazi. Because of the short summers, many of the local vegetables – carrots, beetroot, tomatoes – were pickled, to be eaten during the winter months. Although fish was plentiful (carp and perch from the rivers, cod, herring and sole from the sea), meat still formed the basis for main meals. The traditional menu for Friday night was typically Ashkenazi, with boiled gefilte fish, roast stuffed veal (page 116), potatoes and carrot tzimmes, followed by compote and plava.

POLAND

Jewish population: 1933,   *3,500,000 approx.*
**   1992,**   *6,000*

Although Jews had lived in Poland since the ninth century, in 1264 the Statute of Kalisz officially invited Jews to Poland to help redevelop the country after the Tartar invasions. By 1386, however, the situation had deteriorated and since then the pendulum has swung between periods of great prosperity and freedom, and periods of cruel persecution and even expulsion.

During the sixteenth and seventeenth centuries Jewish communities stabilised; culture and scholarship flourished; there were major developments in Talmudic learning and Rabbinic studies; and there was a creative period in Yiddish language and literature. It was in this atmosphere that Cabbalistic studies developed into Chassidic mysticism.

At the end of the eighteenth century, Poland was divided between Austria, Prussia and Russia, with the majority of Jews living in the Russian-occupied area (the Pale of Settlement). In the nineteenth century many Jews prospered financially but lived in an era of growing anti-semitism that culminated in the pogroms and which, in turn, during the 1880s and after, led to massive emigration to the West, particularly to the Americas.

The Jews were finally given official recognition in 1919 and by 1922, 36 Jews were members of Parliament. A month after the German invasion of September 1939, all Jews in Poland were confined to ghettos. Extermination camps were established in Poland and Jews were brought from all over Europe to be murdered. During the war 3,000,000 Polish Jews died, despite brave resistance both with the partisans and in many ghettos, particularly that of Warsaw.

After the war, Jews who had escaped to the USSR were repatriated. However, the severe outbreaks of anti-semitism that have occurred persistently in Poland (particularly in 1946 and 1967) have resulted in all but 6,000 to 8,000 Jews emigrating, mainly to Israel. In the 1990s there has been some revival of Jewish life and cultural and religious activities. A course in Jewish studies is now available at university level and some synagogues have been restored.

Along with Germany, Poland epitomised Ashkenazi food with warm, comforting dishes such as thick soups much in evidence (see soup section). Gefilte fish (page 97) – referred to as 'the most identifiable dish of the Ashkenazi kitchen' – always had the addition of sugar (sometimes raisins) in Poland, whereas Russian Jews preferred their gefilte fish peppery. Russian influence can be seen, however, in the popularity of borscht (page 91) and kasha (page 151). Chulent with dumplings (page 104) is one of the many Polish chulent recipes that were used for the main Shabbat meal.

SOVIET UNION/RUSSIA

Jewish population: 1933, *2,670,000*
                       1992, *1,400,000*

There were no Jews in the Russian Empire until after the second half of the eighteenth century when large areas of Poland and Lithuania were annexed. Hundreds of thousands of Jews then came under Russian rule but were largely confined to the Pale of Settlement. Here they suffered poverty, overcrowding and a total lack of opportunity for any self-improvement. After the assassination of Alexander II in 1881, the government adopted an openly anti-Jewish policy of savage, organised pogroms, causing many Jews to emigrate or to join revolutionary movements.

One of the first acts of the Revolutionary Provisional Government in 1917 was to abolish all legal restrictions against Jews. Although pogroms continued (100,000 were massacred in the Ukraine), for the first time Jews had the possibility of advancement, which they grasped. By the 1970s Soviet Jewry was described as a scientific and technical elite with Jews in leading roles as doctors, scientists, writers, artists, lawyers, etc. However, Communism virtually destroyed religious life and the rate of assimilation was very fast.

In 1941 the Nazis invaded, occupying the area of the old Pale of Settlement. The approximate number of Jews murdered in the German-conquered areas of the USSR was 2,350,000. During the 1980s and early 1990s the emigration of Jews out of the Soviet Union has grown from a trickle to a flood, the majority going to Israel.

Although there are Sephardi Jews in Georgia and the Central Asian areas of the former Soviet Union, 95 per cent of the Jews are Ashkenazi and this, of course, is reflected in their food. Hot, nourishing soups (page 89) and calf's foot jelly (page 72) were extremely popular and the traditional Russian recipes of borscht and cheese blintzes (page 169) were adopted by the Jewish community. A typical Friday night menu might consist of gefilte fish (page 97), chicken soup, chicken or goose and fruit compote.

Southern Europe

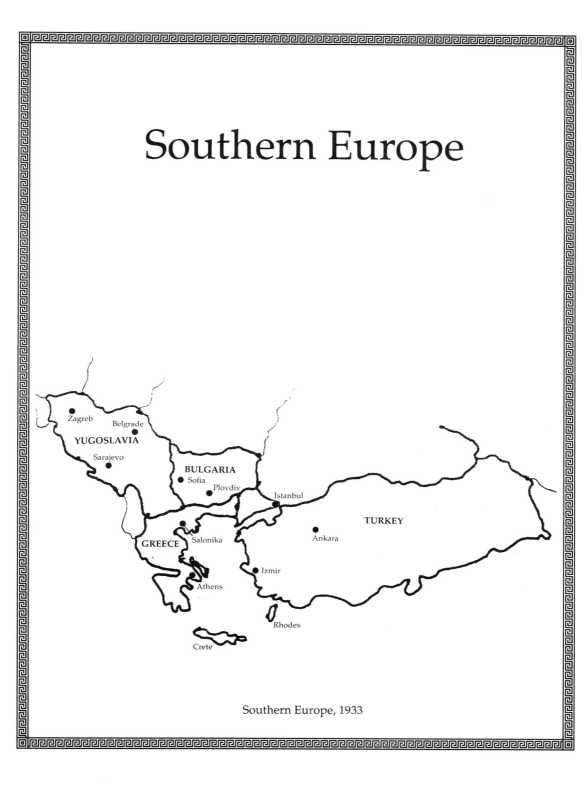

Southern Europe, 1933

BULGARIA

Jewish population: 1933, *46,000*
1992, *4,000*

There were small Jewish communities in Bulgaria during the Roman era. There was an influx of Jews escaping Byzantine persecution during the eighth and ninth centuries, and, in the thirteenth century, a further influx of Jews from Central Europe, fleeing the crusades. In the fourteenth century the Bulgar Tsar married a Jewess who then changed her name from Sarah to Theodora. A further immigration of Jews escaping the Spanish Inquisition occurred in the sixteenth century, creating the important Sephardi Romaniot communities in Sophia, Nicopolis and Plovdiv. Thereafter Ashkenazi and Sephardi communities lived peacefully and independently side by side.

On attaining independence from the Ottoman Empire in 1878, all national minorities were granted equal rights, although there was still a certain amount of anti-semitism. During the Second World War, although Jews from Thrace and Macedonia, areas which had been acquired by Bulgaria in 1940, were deported to concentration camps, Bulgarian Jewry was saved through the intervention of both the King and Bulgarian Church leaders – a rare occurrence in Jewish history. At the end of the Second World War, emigration to Israel became the aim of Bulgarian Jewry and by 1949, 45,000 Jews had made aliyah. The community today is mainly Sephardi; the majority are well-educated professionals and many are involved in the Arts. The rate of inter-marriage is now at 85 per cent.

The recipe for fried brains croquettes (page 115) in this book is evidence of the need in many communities, particularly the poorer, to use all permitted parts of the animal. A similar dish is served by Libyan and Italian Jews.

GREECE

Jewish population: 1928 census, *72,790*
1992, *5,000*

There were Jews in Greece long before the Common Era. By the first and second centuries CE there were large, flourishing communities in Crete, Athens, Corinth and Thessaloniki. After the Spanish Inquisition (1492) many Jews fled to countries which were part of the Ottoman Empire, where they were made welcome. This included Greece and especially Salonika where, by 1613, Jews comprised 68 per cent of the population. Its members became 'Judaised', with all shops and businesses closing on Saturdays and Jewish Holy Days. It became known as the Jerusalem of the Balkans.

During the nineteenth century almost all the ancient original Jewish communities in the Peloponnese were destroyed. In 1917 Greece entered the First World War and later that year a fire destroyed virtually the whole of the Jewish Quarter of Salonika, including all its archives. During the Second World War when Mussolini's army attacked Greece, many Jews helped to defend the Greek borders, but in 1941 the Germans invaded and by the end of the war approximately 65,000 Jews had been deported to concentration camps.

The present-day food served by Greek Jews reflects the ancient roots of the community (the communities on Rhodes and Crete may go back 2,300 years). Culinary influences have been manifold: Roman, Byzantine, Persian, Arab, Spanish and Ottoman. A typical Sabbath evening meal would invariably consist of hamin eggs, beef with bulgar wheat, or casseroled poultry. Sutlach (page 180) is a traditional delicacy served late in the afternoon or after the end of Sabbath. On Rosh Hashana, after the blessing over the apple and honey (which was served in the form of apple and honey jam), the Greeks of Salonika served small portions of three different types of sfongato (page 145) made with finely chopped leeks, grated courgettes and chopped aubergines. A separate blessing was said before each one.

TURKEY

Jewish population: 1933, *81,500*
                  1992, *23,000*

The first Jewish community recorded under Turkish rule was that of Bursa in 1326. In the following century the communities of Salonika and Constantinople came under Turkish occupation. Following the expulsion from Spain in 1482, Jews were invited to settle in the lands of the Ottoman Empire and flourishing communities developed in Istanbul, Izmir and Edirna. The influence of the Sephardi Jews on the original 'Romanide' communities was overwhelming and Ladino became the language used by Turkish Jews.

In 1856 non-Muslims were given the same rights as Muslims, but during the Second World War, when Turkey supported the Axis powers, Jews were unfairly taxed and often imprisoned. These tax laws were repealed in 1944 and defaulters were released. Between 1948 and 1950 about 37,000 Jews emigrated to Israel. The community is mainly Sephardi and approximately 20,000 live in Istanbul.

The climate and agriculture is similar to that of Greece and the cooking of the Jewish community bore great similarity to that of other Sephardi communities in the area.

YUGOSLAVIA

Jewish population: 1933,   *68,400*
              1992,   *5,500*

Jews have lived in the area of Yugoslavia since Roman times, and by medieval times there were various communities along the Dalmatian coast. A number of Spanish Jews sought refuge in Belgrade and Sarajevo after the Inquisition. The area at this time was under Turkish rule and the community continued to speak Ladino until the present century. There were communities of Ashkenazi Jews, particularly in Zagreb, but Jews had restricted rights until 1873. The Ashkenazi community was increased by Jews from Austro-Hungary after the First World War.

Germany invaded Yugoslavia in 1941 and although many Jews fought with the partisans and others were helped to escape, approximately 80 per cent of the population was killed in the Holocaust. In the years after the establishment of the State of Israel a further 9,000 Jews emigrated to Israel. The community today is divided almost equally between Ashkenazi and Sephardi, the largest centres of Jewish population being in Belgrade, Zagreb and Sarajevo.

The cooking reflected the division of the Jewish community in Yugoslavia, with Ashkenazi dishes like ala alas (stuffed carp, page 93) side by side with the Sephardi aros de leci (page 167). Yugoslavia's geographical position enabled the cultivation of fruits such as peaches, apricots, walnuts and almonds as well as apples and plums. A Friday night supper typically featured fish as the main dish, perhaps preceded by a fish soup and followed by a milky pudding such as aros di leci.

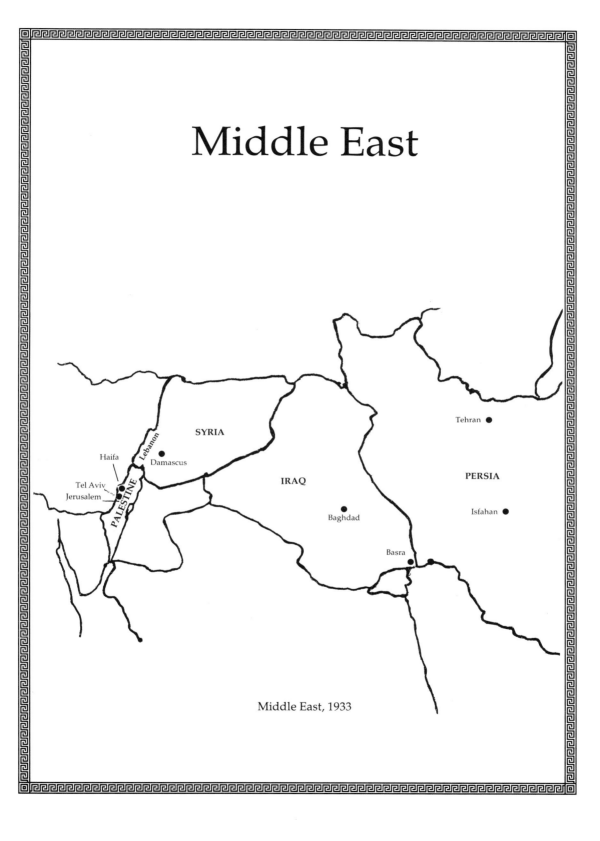

Middle East

SYRIA

Haifa

Tel Aviv

Jerusalem

PALESTINE

Lebanon

Damascus

IRAQ

Baghdad

Basra

Tehran

PERSIA

Isfahan

Middle East, 1933

IRAN/PERSIA

Jewish population: 1933, *40,000*
                      1992, *25,000*

The Persian Jewish community is one of the oldest in the Diaspora, dating back to after the destruction of the First Temple in 538 BCE. Aramaic became the official language of Persia and was adopted by the Jews in religious texts. By the third century CE Jews were experiencing intermittent persecution which was lifted only after the Arab invasion in 642 CE when Jews prospered greatly as weavers, silversmiths and merchants. Many Jews were later forced to convert to Islam when Shi'ism became the dominant form of the Persian Muslim religion.

The communities in Persia became poor and suffered oppression throughout the centuries. However, in this century, as a result of the work of the Alliance Israélite Universelle and later the oil boom, the position of the Jews improved enormously and many of them became very wealthy, although since the revolution of 1979 half the Jewish population has emigrated.

Over the centuries Iranian Jewish cooking has adopted the character of the national cuisine. Rice is pre-eminent, cooked and eaten with poultry (jewelled rice, page 132), with vegetables (rice with broad beans and dill, page 157) and even with fruit. Iranian cookery makes great use of herbs and spices, particularly nutmeg, saffron and cardamom but the overall effect is subtle rather than hot or sharp. Comparatively little use was made of meat or fat. Chicken soup – particularly when served with gondi (page 79) – was a traditional Friday night starter.

IRAQ

Jewish population: 1933, *87,500*
                      1992,   *200*

Ur in southern Iraq was the birthplace of Abraham in about 2000 BCE. The oldest of all Diaspora communities was established in 586 BCE after the destruction of the First Temple, when Nebuchadnezzar conquered Judea and the Jews went into exile. The Jews of Iraq/Babylonia produced some of the greatest scholars and one of the greatest works of Judaism – the Babylonian Talmud. Between the ninth and seventeenth centuries their fortunes fluctuated with the different political situations in Iraq. In the twelfth century CE Benjamin of Tudela reported 40,000 Jews in Baghdad, with at least 28 synagogues and many centres of learning. Under Turkish rule, particularly in the eighteenth and nineteenth centuries, repressive measures resulted in large numbers of Baghdadi Jews emigrating to India and the Far East. The Jewish population during the British mandate in Iraq numbered 100,000.

Kitchen of girls' school in Baghdad, 1930s (from the Gubbay Family Archives).

During and after the Second World War there were fierce anti-Jewish riots and pogroms in Baghdad but after the establishment of the State of Israel, emigration was prohibited, although many Jews did escape through Iran and Turkey. In 1950–51 the government of Israel, together with the Jewish Agency, airlifted 113,545 Iraqi Jews to safety. Most of the remainder of the community were allowed to emigrate only because of the international outrage at the public hangings and secret executions of Jews following the Six Day War.

Iraqi Jewry had a highly developed and sophisticated cuisine which has had a strong influence in the many countries to which Iraqi Jews have emigrated (particularly India and the Sudan). Iraqi Jewish cooking reflected and adapted the mainstream cookery of the Iraqi Arabs. The main Shabbat dish of tebid or tabiyeet (page 136) epitomised the Sephardi version of the Ashkenazi chulent – a meal that was prepared on Friday, put to cook just before the onset of the Sabbath and then cooked slowly until it was ready to be eaten at the end of the Sabbath morning service. Whereas Ashkenazi chulent usually consisted of beef (occasionally goose) with beans and potatoes, tebid (also called hameem (page 131), haminado and dfeena (page 105)) used chicken or mutton with chickpeas and rice. Whole eggs were cooked in the same pot (page 135) and often eaten for breakfast on the Sabbath.

ISRAEL/PALESTINE

**Jewish population: 1933,   *175,000*
                    1992,   *3,755,000***

The first Jewish State was established some 3,000 years ago. With the destruction of the Second Temple in 70 CE and the end of the Bar Kochba revolt, the Jews as a people were dispersed throughout the world. There were, however, always Jews living in the Land of Israel, and the Jewish population increased steadily from the time of the Ottoman conquest in the sixteenth century. The first modern Jewish village, Petach Tikva, was founded in 1878 and immigration to Palestine, particularly by young Zionists from Russia and Eastern Europe, at the end of the eighteenth and the beginning of the nineteenth centuries was substantial; by 1914 there were approximately 85,000 Jews living in Palestine. In 1918 the British were given the mandate to rule Palestine.

With the rise of Nazi power in Germany, many more Jews fled to Palestine, although immigration was severely restricted by the British authorities and continued to be so, even after the Second World War. By 1948, when Israel declared independence, the Jewish population was 650,000. Since then, there have been massive waves of immigrants from all over the world, particularly from North Africa and the Arab countries, and lately, of course, from the Communist countries of Europe, particularly the Soviet Union.

The food in Israel reflects influences from all the different communities of the world now settled there. In the 1930s, the food of the Jews living in Palestine was divided into two distinct styles: the Ashkenazi traditions of the immigrants from Eastern Europe and the Sephardi traditions of the Jews from Turkey and Yemen as well as those who had been settled there for generations. The main fruits were citrus, grapes and olives; apples and pears were hardly available, and there were no avocados at all. Tomatoes, potatoes, carrots and aubergines were all grown in the area.

SYRIA

**Jewish population: 1933,   *26,050* (Syria and Lebanon)
                    1992,   *4,000***

There were Jewish communities living in the area of Syria before the Greek conquest of the fourth century BCE. By the twelfth century CE there were approximately 6,500 Jews, mainly in Damascus, Aleppo and Palmyra. Refugees from Spain, fleeing the Inquisition, settled there at the end of the fifteenth and early sixteenth centuries. Thereafter, the area became part of the Ottoman Empire until the First World War.

In 1840 Damascus was the scene of a notorious blood libel in which many leading Jews were arrested and tortured and although in 1918, under the French occupation,

Jews were given equal rights, anti-Zionist feeling led to fierce outbreaks of violence in which a number of Jews were killed. In the late 1940s many Jews emigrated, mainly to Israel, until a ban was imposed on emigration. The situation deteriorated after the Six Day War, with pogroms and further restrictions, including a limitation on movement and bans on ownership of radios and telephones. The present community is Sephardi and lives in segregated ghettoes in Damascus.

The cooking of Syrian Jews is inextricably linked to the Sephardi communities of the whole region, with influences from Arab and Ottoman traditions, as well as, here, from France. The abundance of vegetables in the area has led to a plethora of fine dishes, particularly vegetables stuffed either with rice or minced meat. Lamb and poultry are the most commonly used meats, many recipes utilising the pounding or mincing of the meat until very finely ground (for example, kibbeh, page 124).

Africa

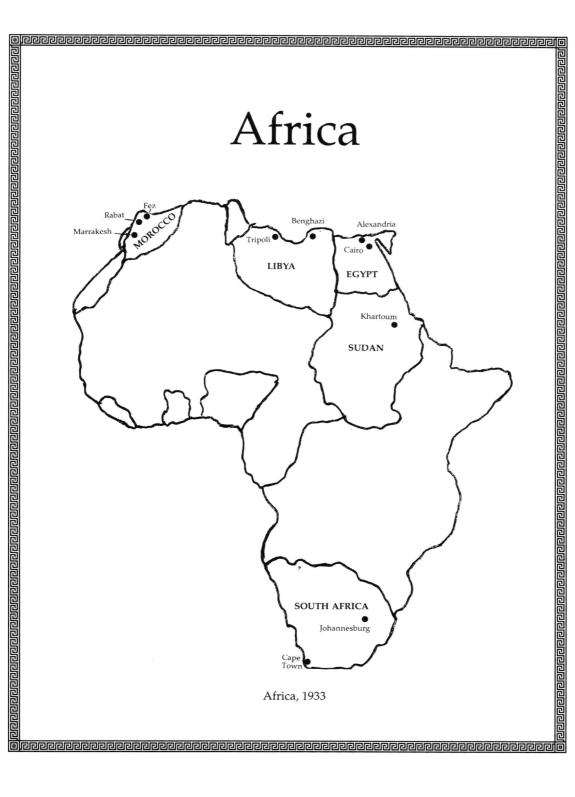

Africa, 1933

EGYPT

Jewish population: 1933,   *63,500*
**   1992,**   *300*

The Jewish community in Egypt dates back to Biblical times. By the start of the Common Era there were 1,000,000 Jews in Egypt, with 332 synagogues in Alexandria alone. It was a major centre for Jewish learning. During the period 20 BCE to 40 CE there was anti-Jewish rioting, and the situation deteriorated further after the Christianisation of the Roman Empire. Pressure was put on the Jews to convert and there was a mass baptism in 415 CE at Alexandria, after which the community dwindled. In the tenth century, a new community was established in Cairo in which Moses Maimonides settled in 1165. Here he wrote much of his work, becoming head of Egyptian Jewry, an honour which was passed down through his family for the next 200 years.

Jews lived uneventfully in Egypt until the twentieth century when anti-Western and particularly anti-Zionist feeling developed. In 1945, ten Jews were killed and many were injured, and at the outbreak of Israel's War of Independence, 2,000 Jews were arrested and their property was confiscated. Some 35,000 Jews emigrated during the years between Israel's War of Independence and the Suez crisis. In 1956, at the start of the Suez crisis, 40,000 Jews were living in Egypt but by 1957 the number had decreased to 15,000. By the time of the Six Day War in 1967 it had dropped to 2,500. Jewish rights were restored after the Sadat/Begin peace negotiations in 1979.

Reflecting the antiquity of their roots in Egypt, the Jewish community adopted the main characteristics of Arab Egyptian cuisine, with a plethora of stuffed vegetables (mahshi), ful (beans) and rice dishes. The most popular Friday night meal was chicken, either casseroled with turmeric and lemon potatoes (page 129) or roasted, with egg and lemon sauce. This was invariably preceded by chicken soup and sometimes accompanied by rice and vermicelli, the latter first fried or grilled then mixed with the rice. A bowl of salad (tomatoes, cucumber, sweet peppers) was always served and dessert was most likely to be fresh fruit or small pastries stuffed with dates. Dfeena (page 105) was the traditional Sabbath day dish.

LIBYA

Jewish population: 1933,   *24,342*
**   1992,**   *20*

The first Jewish settlement was in the Benghazi area in the third century BCE. In the fifteenth century numbers were increased dramatically by Spanish Jews fleeing the Inquisition. Between 1911 and 1936, under Italian occupation, the community prospered greatly until Mussolini introduced anti-Jewish laws. By 1941, 25 per cent of the population of Tripoli was Jewish. After the invasion of 1942, the Germans occupied the Jewish quarter of Benghazi; 2,000 Jews were deported across the desert, very few of whom survived. From the end of the Second World War, Jews were subjected to extreme brutality and were frequently murdered. Most Jews had emigrated to Israel by 1951. After the Six Day War in 1967, there were further murders and destruction of property.

There are Italian as well as North African influences in Libyan Jewish cooking – plenty of pasta and stews as well as the national dish of couscous. As in many North African countries, couscous (page 150) formed the traditional Friday night dish. It was served on the Sabbath with lubia (page 106) – a Libyan 'chulent' – and small stuffed vegetables. These items would be put in a 'cannun', a large clay pot filled with charcoal, which was lit on Friday afternoon and would stay alight until Shabbat lunch, so that the food cooked gently. Whole eggs would be cooked in with the meat.

MOROCCO

Jewish population: 1933, *135,000*
                    1992, *13,000*

Jews have been in the northern part of Morocco since Roman times. Under Muslim rule they experienced alternating periods of tolerance and persecution, with seats of learning established in the eleventh century, notably at Fez, which became a Jewish spiritual centre. Great numbers of refugees arrived from the Iberian peninsula after the Spanish Inquisition, many of the Marranos reconverting on arrival in Morocco. They became farmers, craftsmen and traders in beeswax or ostrich feathers, among other things. In many cities Jews were confined to separate areas known as 'mellahs' which were not dissimilar in effect to European ghettos. Although individual Jews gained prominence in Morocco, the majority were poor and, as non-Muslims, were heavily taxed.

Under the French Protectorate (1912) things began to improve and the community became influenced by French culture. In this century the Casablanca community increased in prosperity and importance. During the Second World War, although under Vichy Rule, the Moroccan King prevented the deportation of Jews. By 1948 the community had reached its peak of 280,000. After the establishment of the State of Israel there were demonstrations of anti-semitism and between 1948 and 1968 almost 176,000 Jews emigrated to Israel and there were further emigrations to France. Jews gained equal rights with Moroccan Independence in 1956.

Moroccan cuisine is one of the great cuisines of the world, taking as it does influences from Arab and French traditions, and the variety and subtlety of Jewish Moroccan food reflected this. French vegetables (artichokes, courgettes and aubergines) and salads were plentiful as were fish, meat and, of course, a rich variety of fruits (dates, belinsi, plums and pears). There was little tradition of dairy foods, while cheese was virtually non-existent. Friday night dinner, as in Jewish communities throughout the world, would have had a fish dish followed by a meat dish (stewed beef or chicken with onions, parsley and saffron) and preceded by chicken soup served with vermicelli which had been grilled, or with a mixture of egg and lemon. The Sabbath dish of dfeena (page 105) would sometimes substitute a whole tongue for the beef and would often be served with a type of large 'sausage' made from rice, minced meat and spices, which would be cooked in the same pot. The dfeena in the northern town of Fez tended to be spicier and hotter than that of Marrakesh, which was sweetened with the addition of burnt sugar. Unlike other North African communities, in Morocco couscous was not a traditional Friday night dish.

SOUTH AFRICA

Jewish population: 1933,   71,800
                    1992,   120,000

There is evidence that Jews went to South Africa with the Portuguese navigators in the seventeenth century, but it was in 1806, under British occupation, that freedom of religion was granted and a community was established in Cape Town in 1841. In the early years of this century there was a large wave of Jewish immigrants from Lithuania (approximately 40,000 Jews) and their descendants still form the majority in the Jewish community. In more recent years – since the 1950s – many thousands of Jews have emigrated from South Africa to Western Europe, Israel and North America. The community is mainly Ashkenazi, well-educated and middle-class.

The cooking is basically traditional Ashkenazi, with herring and kichel, gefilte fish, 'baska' (kuchen), fruit salad and ice-cream cake served for the Sabbath meal.

SUDAN

Jewish population: 1930s,   100 families
                    1992,   1 family

Jews settled in the Sudan for the first time in the early part of the twentieth century. They came mainly from Iraq, Syria and Egypt and they were all of Sephardi origin. Most of the families lived in the capital, Khartoum, with some in Omdurman and Port Sudan. The community consisted mainly of business people who came initially to work for large companies which were intending to expand in the Sudan, but they soon began to set up their own businesses. Most of the community were fairly prosperous and the children were well educated at English or missionary schools. English was the main language spoken, with Arabic as the second.

There was one synagogue in Khartoum and its community was very close-knit although not particularly observant. However, they all kept kosher homes and many kept the Sabbath strictly. The High Holydays were observed and all Jewish shops closed. Kosher meat was available, but the shochet would come to people's homes to slaughter chickens. Most of the community began to leave the Sudan in the 1950s.

The community ate mainly Sephardi-style food and the main meal was always at lunch time and consisted of lamb or veal (very rarely beef which was classed as a poor man's food). In the evenings they served lighter meals which were mainly milky, such as eggahs (omelettes), fried fish and cheeses. A typical Friday night dinner would be fried fish and a Sabbath lunch would be mahshi (stuffed vegetables) and probably roast lamb. At Pesach they would eat roast lamb and rice. Rice was served with every meal. As there were no kosher foods such as jams, cheeses, etc. available, everything had to be made at home using fresh ingredients. Only matzo meal was imported and it normally came from Egypt or England.

Asia

INDIA

Calcutta

● Bombay

Cochin ●

SUMATRA

BORNEO

DUTCH EAST INDIES

Jakarta — ● JAVA ●
Surabaya

Asia, 1933

INDIA

Jewish population: 1933,   *24,000*
**   1992,   *5,600***

Although Jews probably settled in India after the Common Era, the first historical evidence of Jews in India is from 1,000 CE, when the leader of the Jewish community in the Malabar coast was granted certain privileges by the local Hindu ruler. The Jews of India can be divided into three distinct groups:

(1) The Cochin Jews, consisting of two different communities: (a) the Black Jews or Malabaris (population 1,000 in the twelfth century) who regarded themselves as the descendants of the original settlers and were mainly traders and craftsmen; and (b) the White Jews, descendants of Jews who went to India in the sixteenth and seventeenth centuries from Europe and the Middle East (there are about 90 White Jews today as the majority have emigrated to Israel);

(2) The Bene Israel claim to have arrived in India in the second century BCE. They adopted the customs and dress of their local Hindu and Muslim neighbours, spoke the local language and gave up many Jewish practices. They were farmers and oil pressers but refused to work on the Sabbath; they also retained certain traditions, including the basic dietary laws and circumcision. They remained isolated until discovered by the Jews of Cochin in the late sixteenth century. They comprise the largest Jewish community in India and are based in Bombay;

(3) The Baghdadi Jews who arrived in India during the nineteenth and twentieth centuries. They became a prosperous community, active in the civic and commercial life of Bombay and Calcutta. In the early years they retained their Arabic language, although they came to identify with the British rulers and later adopted English as their mother tongue.

The 'tripartite' division of Indian Jewry is reflected in their cooking. The food of the Bene Israel was indistinguishable from that of the native population. The Cochin Jews, although influenced by Iraqi cuisine, ate much hotter, spicier food and used the local coconut harvest for both cooking oil and milk. The Baghdadi Jews retained their Middle Eastern style of cooking, although they gradually incorporated local ingredients and dishes (particularly the breads). The use of poultry and fish was far more prevalent in Calcutta homes since there were few facilities for the slaughter of large animals in Hindu areas. A typical Friday night meal might include aloo makala (page 153), pot roast chicken (page 128) and halwa (page 214), and Sabbath lunch would consist of hameem, cooked overnight (page 131).

INDONESIA/DUTCH EAST INDIES

Jewish population: 1933,   *900*
              1945,   *3,000*
              1992,   *16*

In the nineteenth century Jews from Baghdad and Holland came to the Dutch East Indies for commercial reasons. They settled mainly in Surabaya which was an important trading port. There was also a community in Jakarta (although the only synagogue is in Surabaya) and a small community living in Aceh in northern Sumatra. Between the two World Wars there was an influx of Jews from Germany and Eastern Europe. In 1942, after the Japanese invasion, all Europeans were put into concentration camps. After the war and with the independence of Indonesia in 1949, most Jews left for Australia and the US. There are now many Western people living temporarily in Indonesia who are largely involved in the textile industry.

The cooking of the Jews in Indonesia was based on the traditions of the original communities (Ashkenazi for the Dutch Jews and Sephardi for the Baghdadis), although both groups adapted to the local conditions and produce, especially in the use of fruits such as mangoes, bananas and pineapples.

The Americas

CANADA

Winnipeg

Toronto Ottawa
Montreal

U.S.A.

Chicago New York

Los Angeles

MEXICO

Miami

Mexico
City

JAMAICA

ARGENTINA

Buenos
Aires

The Americas, 1933

ARGENTINA

Jewish population: 1933, *215,000*
1992, *300,000*

The earliest Jewish settlers in Argentina were Marranos in the sixteenth century, but they assimilated. The modern community dates from the middle of the last century, coming mainly from Germany and Central Europe, and from Eastern Europe in 1889. Refugees fleeing the Nazis settled in Argentina in the 1930s and there was further immigration after the Second World War. Under the military regime (1976–83) many Jews emigrated, mainly to the US, Israel and Spain. Eighty-five per cent of the present community are Ashkenazi and fifteen per cent Sephardi, who came mainly from the Middle East. A small number of Jews live in rural areas as a result of a programme by the Jewish Colonisation Association in 1892.

Reflecting the dominance of the Ashkenazi culture within the community, cooking for traditional celebrations is very similar to that of Europe. In Argentina the emphasis is on roast and grilled meats, roast chicken being the favourite Friday night dinner.

CANADA

Jewish population: 1933, *155,600*
1992, *325,000*

Jews were banned from Canada during the period of French rule. The first synagogue was a Sephardi synagogue in Montreal in the early 1770s, although Ashkenazi Jews were among its founders. An Ashkenazi synagogue was established in 1856 in Toronto. The first Jew was elected to the Quebec Assembly in 1807 but was not allowed to take his seat. The Jewish community increased considerably with the immigration of Jews from Eastern Europe at the end of the last century. There are flourishing communities in Montreal and Toronto, Winnipeg and Vancouver, as well as many smaller communities.

Cooking among the Jews in Canada reflected the origins of the members of each community, which means a largely Ashkenazi cuisine. Because of the availability of good fresh meat, brisket was baked rather than pickled (page 103) and a lokshen kugel was a popular accompaniment to the main course. The most popular North American recipe adopted by the Jews in Canada seems to have been muffins. Blueberry muffins (page 188) were served to guests in the 1930s – and still are. A typical Friday night meal might have been gefilte fish or chopped liver, chicken soup, roast chicken with noodle pudding (page 153) and tzimmes, followed by an apple pudding.

JAMAICA

Jewish population: 1933, *1,250*
1992,   *800*

The first Jews to settle in Jamaica were probably Marranos in the sixteenth century, followed by more Sephardim in the seventeenth century, after the British occupation of the island in 1655. The Ashkenazi community comprised mainly English Jews in the eighteenth century. Full equality was granted to Jewish citizens in 1831, earlier than in England itself. At its peak, the community had synagogues in Montego Bay, Spanish Town and Port Royal, but during the later nineteenth and early twentieth centuries the numbers of Jews dwindled and the Ashkenazi and Sephardi communities combined to form a single community in 1921 in Kingston. After the granting of independence in 1962 many Jews emigrated, fearing a Communist takeover. The community is further declining through assimilation.

The island is extremely fertile producing a variety of fruits and vegetables, particularly mangoes, plantains, cabbage, peppers and tomatoes. All these were in plentiful supply, as were fish and poultry.

MEXICO

Jewish population: 1933, *16,000*
1992, *35,000*

In the early years of the sixteenth century Marrano Jews went to Mexico and in the final years of the last century there was an influx of Syrian Jews from Aleppo. However, most of the Jewish population of Mexico originated in the US. There are now both Sephardi and Ashkenazi congregations. The majority of Mexico's Jews live in Mexico City, with small communities in Acapulco and elsewhere.

Cooking in Mexico is influenced by Creole and Indian traditions. It tends to be very spicy (chillies are used frequently) and most dishes are served with a sauce. Avocados, tomatoes and carob are among the main crops.

UNITED STATES OF AMERICA

Jewish population: 1933,   *4,228,000*
                1992,   *5,950,000*

The first recorded community in America was in New Amsterdam in 1654, although there were definitely Jews in Columbus's crew in 1492. The first synagogue was consecrated in New York in 1730. With the granting of Independence in 1776, freedom of religion was given to all states except Maryland and North Carolina. In the late nineteenth century there was an influx of German and Polish immigrants and in the 30 years after 1882, two million Jews emigrated to America, mostly from Eastern Europe. Jews fleeing the Nazi persecutions further increased the American Jewish population and by the end of the war the US had become the centre of world Jewry.

The highest concentration of Jews is on the Eastern seaboard with nearly two million Jews in and around New York. The community plays a major role in the cultural, academic and business life of the nation as well as in its politics. Although there are centres throughout the US where Jewish life is vibrant and flourishing, less than half of American Jews are affiliated to synagogues and the rate of inter-marriage is high. The community is mainly Ashkenazi although, in recent years, there have been influxes of Jews from Iran and there are large communities of Israelis in New York and Los Angeles.

America, known as the land of plenty, offered its immigrants a wealth of different foods. In the absence of a characteristic American cuisine, many communities in the inter-war years continued to cook the traditional dishes of their parents and grandparents. A famous cookbook – *The Settlement Cook Book* – first published in 1901 and given to many of the new immigrant Jews, attempted to present an all-American cookery style, with recipes for clams, pork and crab alongside those for cholla (Sabbath twists), matzos and farfel.

Australasia

Australasia, 1933

AUSTRALIA

Jewish population: 1933, *27,000*
1992, *90,000*

The first known Jews in Australia were among the convicts transported from Britain in 1788 when the first penal settlement in Australia was founded. The first voluntary settlers arrived in the 1820s. The great Australian gold rush of the nineteenth century attracted more Jewish immigrants and their number increased steadily until the Second World War. After the war many Jewish refugees from Eastern Europe settled in Australia. There have been two Jewish Governor-Generals. The community is predominantly middle-class Ashkenazi and is one of the few increasing communities in the Diaspora.

The traditional Ashkenazi cooking has been adapted to use locally grown produce. The most commonly grown fruits are canteloupe and water melons, grapes, apples, pears, passion and kiwi fruits and mandarins. Pumpkin was among the most popular vegetables, and meat was home grown and therefore both plentiful and relatively cheap, as was fish, particularly mullet, sole and cod. A typical Friday night meal was chopped liver with new green cucumbers, chicken soup with lokshen and there was often a choice of main courses, such as lamb in honey, roast chicken or smoked brisket. The pumpkin was roasted together with potatoes and onions, and fresh fruit or compote was served for dessert.

INDEX
OF RECIPES
AROUND THE
WORLD

Belgium

Bulgaria

Canada

Czechoslovakia

Greece

Indonesia

Iran/Persia

Iraq

Portugal

Romania

South Africa

Spain

Soviet Union/Russia

INDEX OF FESTIVAL FOOD

SHAVUOT

TISHA B'AV

WEDDINGS

CIRCUMCISION

GLOSSARY OF JEWISH CULINARY TERMS

BAGEL   A ring-shaped bread roll, made from yeast dough which is first boiled and then glazed with egg and baked. Water or egg bagels are most common but onion, rye, pumpernickel, cinnamon-raisin and cheese bagels are other favourites.

BLINTZES   Thin pancakes, Russian in origin but similar to French crêpes, stuffed with various fillings and often topped with sour cream or jam.

BORSCHT   A Russian-style soup that can be served either hot or cold, usually made from various combinations of beetroot, spinach, sorrel, cabbage and meat. Often served with sour cream, boiled potatoes and pickled cucumbers.

CHAROSETH   A mixture of chopped fruits, nuts and spices moistened with wine and eaten during the Seder services on Passover.

CHOLLA   A plaited loaf traditionally made with a yeast egg dough and used for Sabbath and festivals.

CHRANE   The Yiddish word for grated horseradish which usually has beetroot juice added.

CHREMSEL   A Passover fritter made with matzo meal and glazed with honey or a sugar and cinnamon mixture.

CHULENT   A traditional meat and vegetable stew prepared before the Sabbath begins and left to cook slowly overnight and then eaten on the Sabbath.

COMPOTE   A French term that has been adopted by Jewish cooks and refers to a mixture of dried and/or fresh fruits that are sweetened and then cooked.

EINGEMACHT   Traditional Passover preserve of German origin, usually made from beetroot, spices and nuts. Can also be made with carrots.

FALAFEL   A deep-fried chickpea croquette of Middle Eastern origin that is served as an hors d'œuvre or stuffed into the pocket of pitta bread with lettuce and tahini or hummous.

FARFEL   Noodle dough that has been grated or chopped into fine pieces and used as a garnish for soup or meat dishes. Can also be made with matzo.

FLANKEN   Flanken steak is a versatile cut of kosher beef from below the ribs.

FLEISHIG   Food prepared with meat or meat products.

GEFILTE FISH   Gefilte is the German word for stuffed and refers to a mixture of ground fish, matzo meal, eggs and vegetables shaped into balls and then poached in fish broth.

GRIBENES   Chicken cracklings, made from skin, cut up and fried in rendered chicken fat (schmaltz) until crisp, then drained and sprinkled with salt.

HAMANTASCHEN   Triangular pastries filled with poppy seeds, jam, prunes or other mixtures and served at Purim time to resemble the three-cornered hat that Haman used to wear.

HELZEL   Stuffed chicken neck made with a vegetable and bread mixture and then baked.

HOLISHKES   Sweet and sour cabbage leaves stuffed with meat and rice.

HUMMOUS   A Middle Eastern dip made from chickpeas and sesame seed paste.

KARTOFFEL   Potato dumplings or potato croquettes.

KASHA   Buckwheat groats usually served as an accompaniment to meat, but also in soups, salads or as a breakfast cereal.

KNEIDLACH   Also called matzo balls – dumplings made of matzo meal and served in chicken soup or potted meat dishes.

KNISHES   Stuffed dumplings filled with potatoes, meat, cheese or rice and then either fried, boiled or baked.

KREPLACH   Pockets of pasta-like dough that are stuffed with meat or cheese and then boiled in broth or fried – similar to ravioli.

KUGEL Potatoes or noodles combined with an egg mixture and baked in the oven like a pudding. Usually served as a vegetable or, when sweetened with raisins, sugar and apples, as a dessert.

LATKES Small pancakes of potatoes, noodles, vegetables or fruits. Potato latkes fried in oil are a traditional food during Chanukah.

LEKACH Dark honey cake which is traditionally served during Rosh Hashana and Yom Kippur.

LEKVAR A prune preserve used for filling hamantaschen or other pastries.

LOCKSHEN Egg noodles, traditionally served in soup or used in a kugel.

MAMALIGA Cornmeal cooked into a cereal or porridge, served with cheese, sour cream and sugar – originally from Romania.

MANDELBROT Twice-baked crisp almond cookies made in Germany.

MANDLEN A baked dough mixture cut into tiny squares and served in soup.

MATZO Unleavened bread traditionally served during the eight days of Passover.

MATZO BREI An omelette made with matzo.

MATZO CAKE MEAL Matzo that is ground extra finely and used for baking and stuffings.

MATZO MEAL Matzo that is ground finely and used as a substitute for flour during Passover.

MILCHIG Made of milk or dairy products.

MILTZ A spleen which is usually stuffed and baked.

MOHN A poppy seed mixture used for filling hamantaschen and other pastries.

PAREV 'Neutral' food that contains no meat or dairy products and could be eaten with either milchig or fleishig meals.

PERROGEN Also called piroshki, these are Russian-style dumplings that are filled with meat, kasha or liver mixture and then baked.

PITTA BREAD Middle Eastern flat round bread with a pocket that can be filled with falafel, hummous, tahina and salads.

SCHAV   Sorrel, a vegetable used in cold soup or borscht, Russian in origin, and now served in Israel during Shavuot.

SCHMALTZ   Rendered chicken fat which is used instead of butter, margarine or oil.

STREUSEL   Sweet crumb topping for coffee cakes and breads.

STRUDEL   A pastry made of very thin sheets of dough and filled with a variety of sweet and savoury mixtures.

SUFGANIYOT   Deep fried doughnuts served during Chanukah.

TAHINA   Sesame seed paste usually served as a dip or with falafel in a pitta.

TEIGLACH   Dough confections that are boiled in honey.

TZIMMES   A mixture of sweet potatoes, prunes, carrots and assorted dried fruits that are often sweetened and sometimes cooked with meat. From Germany.

VARNISHKES   Noodle dough rolled and shaped into bows, traditionally served with kasha.

RECIPES

STARTERS

Black Olives

RUSSIA   Carol Middleweek

Preparation 15 mins   **Cook 15 mins**   **Advance**

1 lb firm black olives (450 g)   1 small onion sliced
1 average size marrow, seeds removed   2 tomatoes, skinned
Small slice cholla or white breadcrumbs Juice of 1 lemon
Black pepper   Oil for cooking

Stone the olives. Cut the marrow into ½" (1¼ cm) slices. Fry gently until soft. Cook the onion slowly in a little oil until soft. Do not burn. Cook tomatoes for a few minutes until juices have evaporated. Chop all the ingredients into fine pieces. This is not a purée and it is preferable to chop it on a board with a chopper or knife. However, if a food processor is used, process in small amounts for just a split second. Season with a little lemon juice and black pepper. Add enough breadcrumbs to absorb any liquid, but do not make mixture too heavy.

This recipe is from my aunt's family, the Shestopals, who came from Simferopol in the Crimea. It was eaten with cholla and butter at Rosh Hashana and Yom Kippur – to break (not take) the Fast! Makes a wonderful canapé.

Cheese Biscuits

CZECHOSLOVAKIA   Mariette Demuth

Preparation 10 mins   Gas No 2, 300°F, 160°C   Cook 15–20 mins approx   Advance

6–8 oz strong Cheddar cheese, grated   1 egg yolk for glazing
   (170–225 g)   Plain flour, same weight as cheese
Butter or margarine, same weight as cheese Caraway seeds to sprinkle

Beat together cheese, butter and flour. If mixture is too soft leave in fridge for 1 hour. Form mixture into small round balls or ½" × 2" (1 × 5 cm) strips if preferred. Brush with egg yolk and sprinkle with a few caraway seeds. Bake very slowly until light golden brown.

Cheese Savouries

GERMANY   Herta Linden

Preparation 15 mins   **Gas No 6, 400°F, 200°C**   **Cook 10 mins approx**   **Advance**

6 oz plain flour (170 g)   Pinch of salt
4 oz butter or margarine (115 g)   Squeeze of lemon juice
1 tbls icy water   1½ oz cheese, grated (45 g)

Mix ingredients into pastry dough in the normal way. Shape dough into straws or other shapes as desired. Place on greased tin and bake until shapes are crisp and only lightly browned.

Kichels for Baked Herring

SOUTH AFRICA   RSA Union of Jewish Women

Preparation 15 mins   **Gas No 7, 425°F, 220°C**   **Cook 10–15 mins**   **Advance**

½ cup sugar   6 eggs
½ cup oil   1 tsp baking powder
3 cups plain flour

Beat four whole eggs plus *either* two whites or two yolks with the sugar. Add oil, flour and baking powder and mix until it becomes a dough. Roll out thinly and cut into diamond shapes. Place on oiled baking sheet. Prick and bake until golden brown. Cool. (Be careful it does not burn; it breaks easily but broken pieces taste just as good.)

Perrogen

LITHUANIA – VILNA   Pearl Fogell

Serves 4   **Preparation 10 mins**   **Gas No 4, 350°F, 185°C**   **Cook 1 hr approx**

1 lb shortcrust pastry (450 g)   *Filling*
   (made with nut oil or margarine)   Lung and miltz
                                            1 onion, minced or chopped
                                            1 egg
                                            Salt and pepper

Cover the lung and miltz with water (a difficult task as the air in the lung causes it to float), boil until tender. When the meat is cold, mince finely and mix with onion, beaten egg (reserve a small amount to brush over the pastry), salt and pepper. Roll out the pastry fairly thin and cut into 4" (10 cm) squares. Place the meat filling in the middle of the square so that the pastry, after moistening the edges, can be folded over to form a triangle. Brush pastry with the reserved beaten egg. Place pies on a baking tray and bake.

Artichokes with Lemon – Enjinares

GREECE

Serves 8   Preparation 10 mins   Resting time 10 mins   Cook 1 hr approx   Advance

8 artichokes – hearts and stems
Juice of 3 lemons
2 tbls honey
¼ cup olive oil

1½ cups water
Salt and pepper
Chopped dill

Cut the hearts and stems in half and place the artichokes on a large plate with the exposed hearts down. Sprinkle with the juice of one lemon and leave for about 10 minutes. Arrange the artichokes in a large pan – stem side up – and add the water carefully. Then add all the remaining ingredients. Simmer gently, tightly covered, until tender. Serve cold.

This dish is commonly used at Passover, when artichokes are in season.

Carciofi Alla Giudaica

ITALY   Elena Grosskopf

Serves 6   **Preparation 25 mins**   **Cook 25 mins**

6 medium globe artichokes
Juice of ½ lemon
Salt
Freshly ground pepper

Vegetable oil for frying
2 garlic cloves, crushed
Garnish
Parmesan cheese, grated

Remove outer leaves from the artichokes, cut off the tops and then clean out the inner hairy part. Sprinkle a little lemon juice on each artichoke. In a frying pan, simmer the garlic in a little oil for a few minutes. Open the artichokes like a flower and place face down in the pan, sprinkle with salt and pepper and add a little water. Cover and allow to simmer for about 20 minutes. Before serving, sprinkle with Parmesan cheese. Serve hot.

Aubergine Salad

TURKEY/ROMANIA   Loni Eibenschutz

Serves 4   **Preparation 1¼ hrs**

3 large aubergines   1 garlic clove, crushed
Olive oil   Juice of ½ lemon
Salt to taste

Roast aubergines under the grill, turning them frequently, until skin is charred (or bake in the oven for about 1 hour). Put them under cold running water, then peel and mince them. Add salt. Stirring well, gradually add enough olive oil, together with the lemon juice and garlic, to obtain a cream with the consistency of mayonnaise. Makes a delicious dip for cocktails or as an hors d'oeuvre.

In Turkey this dish was traditionally served at Rosh Hashanah. In Romania it is usually served with black or rye bread and sliced tomatoes.

Calf's Foot Jelly I

ENGLAND   Janet Cohen

Preparation 20 mins   **Gas No ½, 250°F, 140°C**   **Cook 10 hrs**   **Refrigerate 3 hrs**

1 calf's foot   2 onions, sliced
Veal bones   2 carrots, sliced
Salt and pepper   2 hard boiled eggs

Clean the calf's foot thoroughly. Cover with water, bring to the boil and add all ingredients except eggs. Skim well and then put in a casserole in a slow oven for 10 hours (do not allow to dry). When cooked, drain through a sieve, pouring strained juices into a pyrex dish. Discard veal bones – cut meat from calf's foot into small pieces and add to juices. Add sliced hard boiled eggs and carrots. Leave to set and serve in slices.

Calf's Foot Jelly II

RUSSIA   Frances Ravden

Serves 4   **Preparation 5 mins**   **Cook 4–6 hrs**   **Advance**

1 calf's foot   1 onion, unskinned
2 eggs, hard boiled   Salt and pepper

Clean calf's foot with hot and cold water, then place in saucepan and cover with cold water, bring to the boil and skim. Add the onion and salt to taste. Cook for 4–6 hours. Remove all bones (reserving stock) then chop meat and add salt and pepper. Slice hard boiled eggs. Put meat into large bowl and mix in a little stock. Divide between four dishes, place slices of egg on top, add rest of stock and leave to set.

Cheese Sumoosuks

INDIA

Serves 4–6   **Preparation 15 mins**   **Standing time 1 hr**   **Cook 15–20 mins**

Dough
1 lb S.R. flour (450 g)
Pinch of salt
3 oz butter, clarified (85 g)
2 tsp vinegar
2 tsp water

Filling
6 oz hard white cheese, grated (170 g)
1 egg, lightly beaten
Salt and pepper
Mustard (optional)
Butter to fry

Dough: Rub butter into flour and salt and bind with vinegar and water. Let dough stand, covered, for 1 hour. Divide dough into large marble-sized balls. Roll out each ball into a circle.

Filling: Mix all filling ingredients together. Then place filling on one side of each dough circle and fold other side of the circle over. Wet the edges and crimp together. Fry in hot butter, spooning the hot butter over the sumoosuks to make them puff up. Serve hot.

Traditionally served at Shevuot by the Jews of Calcutta.

Egg and Onion

POLAND   Greta Goldwater

Serves 3–4   **Preparation 5 mins**

3 hard boiled eggs, chopped
Chicken pupick, heart, liver (which have
   been cooked in chicken soup)

1 onion, finely chopped
Salt and pepper to taste

Chop the pupick, heart and liver and mix together with eggs, onion, salt and pepper. Eat with matzos.

Baked Herring

SOUTH AFRICA   RSA Union of Jewish Women

Serves 4   Soaking time 12 hrs   Preparation 10 mins   Gas No 4, 350°F, 185°C
Cook 35 mins

3 schmaltz/salted herrings   **Cinnamon and sugar**
4–6 onions, sliced   **Butter or margarine**
Oil for frying

Soak herrings in cold water overnight and drain. Fry onions in oil until soft and place them in ovenproof dish. Lay herrings on top. Sprinkle with cinnamon and sugar and dot with butter or margarine. Bake.

Served for Kiddush.

Chopped Herring

RUSSIA   Frances Ravden

Serves 4   Soaking time 12 hrs   Preparation 20 mins   Advance

2 salt herrings   **Vinegar**
Small slice of bread   **Seasoning**
Small Spanish onion, finely chopped   **Sugar**
3 eggs, hard boiled

Soak herrings overnight. Skin them and then wash well. Bone and chop herrings with 1 whole egg and 2 egg whites – reserving the remaining 2 egg yolks. Soak bread in vinegar and add onion, salt, pepper and a little sugar. Mix all ingredients well together. Decorate with the crumbled yolks.

Herring Salad I

GERMANY   Anne Schwab

Serves 8   Soaking time 30 mins   Preparation 15 mins   Refrigerate 24 hrs

6 fillets of matjes herrings   **1 tsp French mustard**
**   (soaked in cold water)**   **1 large beetroot, cooked, peeled and grated**
3 large dessert apples, peeled and grated **4 pickled cucumbers, chopped**
1 cup cooked cranberries   **2 tbls mayonnaise**
1 bay leaf   **½ cup chopped walnuts**

Cut the soaked herrings into pieces and mix with the cucumbers, apples and beetroot. Add the remaining ingredients, mix well and refrigerate for a day. Freezes well.

Herring Salad II

GERMANY　　　　　　　　　　　　　　　　　　　　　Marianne Keats

Serves 4–6　　　**Soaking time 1–2 days**　　　**Preparation 15 mins**　　　**Resting time 2 hrs**

1 lb salted herring (450 g)
2 tbls lemon juice
8 tbls sour cream

½ tbls sugar
6 tbls red-skinned apple, coarsely chopped
1 tbls chopped parsley or chives

Soak herrings in cold water for 1–2 days, changing water frequently. Fillet herrings, removing skin and bones, and then cut into convenient pieces of 1½" × 1" (3 × 2 cms) approximately. Place pieces of fish in a shallow dish. Mix apple, sour cream, lemon juice and sugar and pour over fish. Sprinkle top with parsley or chives and leave for at least two hours before serving. (If red apple is not available, a green apple can be used but then add a little coarsely chopped cooked beetroot for colour.)

Knishes

ROMANIA　　　　　　　　　　　　　　　　　　　　　Bertha Rayner

Serves 4　　　　　　　**Preparation 15 mins**　　　　　　**Cook 30 mins**

Dough
3 large potatoes, peeled and sliced
2 eggs
Salt and white pepper to taste
A little plain flour mixed with a pinch of
　baking powder
Oil for frying

Filling
2 onions, minced
12 oz minced meat (340 g)
Salt and pepper to taste
2 tbls chicken fat or substitute

Dough: Boil potatoes in salted water until soft, remove from heat, drain and mash them, then allow to cool. Add eggs and seasoning. Mix well and add enough flour to make a soft dough.
Filling: Sauté onions in the fat until brown, then stir in minced meat and seasonings and fry until brown.
Roll out the dough and cut into squares. Place a little filling on the centre of each square, fold the dough over and form triangles, sealing the edges well. Deep fry them in oil until golden brown.

Korozot

HUNGARY   Sandra Berzon

Preparation 10 mins   **Refrigerate 1 hr minimum**   **Advance**

5 fl oz natural yoghurt or single cream (145
 ml)
8 oz carton cottage cheese (225 g)
1 clove garlic, crushed
Finely chopped onions, chives or spring
 onions to taste

2oz butter or margarine (55 g)
½ tsp paprika
½ tsp caraway seeds
½ tsp continental mustard

Empty the cottage cheese into a bowl and add all other ingredients. Mix well together
and chill in refrigerator for at least 1 hour. More (or less) paprika, garlic and caraway
seeds may be added according to taste. This is delicious with crackers, as a filling for
tomatoes or in sandwiches.

Chopped Liver Balls

TURKEY   Jane Finestone

Preparation 10 mins   **Cook 5 mins**

1 oz chicken livers (25 g)
1 egg, separated
2 dsp flour

1 tsp fresh parsley, chopped
Salt to taste
1 dsp melted margarine

Chop liver very finely and cream with melted margarine and salt. Add egg yolk and
mix well. Beat egg white stiffly and add with the parsley and flour to liver. Stir gently
but well. Dip a teaspoon into boiling water and spoon out the batter mixture, a
spoonful at a time, into boiling salted water. Cook until the liver balls float. Remove
and drain. They can be boiled in chicken stock if preferred. They can be used in soup or
as a side dish.

Henrek's Chopped Liver Pâté

RUSSIA   Mila Griesel

Serves 16   **Preparation 20 mins**   **Cook 15 mins**   **Advance**

4 lb chicken livers (1.8 kg)
4 large eggs, hard boiled
Chicken schmaltz, kosher margarine or a
 good pure sunflower oil

3 lb English onions, sliced (1.3 kg)
Salt and pepper
3 cloves garlic

Wash livers thoroughly. Fry onions until brown and remove from fat. Add livers to fat
and fry with garlic until just cooked through and remove from fat. Put all ingredients
individually through a coarse-cut food processor and then place in a bowl, add juice
from frying pan, mix together and allow to cool.

Liver Toasties

POLAND   Ray Freedman

Serves 4   **Preparation 10 mins**   **Cook 10 mins**

12 oz chicken livers (340 g)
3 medium Spanish onions, finely sliced
Chicken fat or sunflower oil
1 pinch sugar

3 eggs, hard boiled
4 slices cholla or any other bread
Salt and pepper

Coarsely chop the eggs and reserve. Sauté onions until soft then add chicken livers cut into ¾″ (1.75 cm) pieces. Sprinkle with salt, pepper and a pinch of sugar and sauté until just cooked. Toast the bread and pour a little of the liver gravy over each piece. Cover with the onion rings, then the liver and finally place some of the chopped egg on top. Serve warm.

SOUPS AND ACCOMPANIMENTS

Farfel

CZECHOSLOVAKIA
Jackie Gryn

Serves 4   **Preparation 5 mins**   **Cook 15–20 mins**

½ cup farfel
1½ cups boiling water
½ tsp salt and pepper
1 tbls chicken fat

Heat fat and then add farfel and stir until browned. Pour on boiling water, season and cover. Cook slowly for 15 to 20 minutes. Drain.

Matzo Farfel

POLAND
Rebecca Bonstein

Serves 8–10   **Preparation 5 mins**   **Soaking time 30 mins**   **Gas No 1, 275°F, 150°C**
Cook 30 mins approx

6 matzos
1 to 2 eggs, beaten

Break up matzos into very small pieces. Mix matzo pieces with the egg and leave for 30 minutes. Place pieces on a baking tray in a single layer – do not pile up. Put in the oven for as long as it takes to dry out the egg. Turn pieces every 10 minutes until cooked. Cool and store in plastic bags. When required, cook for 10 minutes in a pan of boiling salted water and then drain and serve in chicken soup.

Gondi

IRAN/PERSIA   Sarah Hai

Serves 6   **Preparation 20 mins**   **Cook 3 hrs**

8 oz minced beef or chicken (225 g)   *Stock*
8 oz chickpeas (225 g), soaked overnight   3 pints water (1½ litres)
1 medium onion   Chicken wings or meat bones
1 tbls chicken fat or margarine   2 sticks celery
½ tsp ground cumin   ½ onion
½ tsp ground cardamom   ¼ tsp turmeric powder
1 egg, beaten   Salt and pepper
Salt and pepper

Make a meat stock by boiling stock ingredients together for 2 hours. Mince the drained chickpeas. Add the minced meat, onion and chicken fat or margarine and mince it all together. Place the mixture in a bowl. Add the egg, spices, salt and pepper and mix with a fork. Make into balls (a little larger than golf balls), put them into the strained stock and cook for 1 hour.

Gondi are specially made by Persian Jews to be eaten on Friday night or Saturday. They can be eaten on their own or with chicken soup and rice. They are also served with drinks at parties.

Grapeleck

POLAND   Greta Goldwater

Preparation 10 mins   **Cook 2 mins**

½ pint water (¼ litre)   Salt
2 oz semolina (55 g)

Bring water to boil, add semolina and salt to taste. Cook, stirring constantly, until mixture thickens. Turn onto plates and leave to set. When cold, cut into small squares.

Griessnockerl – Semolina Dumplings

AUSTRIA   Ruth Smilg

Serves 6   **Preparation 10 mins**   **Standing time 1 hr**   **Cook 15–20 mins**   **Advance**

1 tbls chicken fat   4 tbls coarse semolina
1 egg, lightly beaten   Pinch of salt and pepper

Cream fat, gradually add semolina, egg, salt and pepper. Leave for 1 hour. Scoop out small balls with a teaspoon and drop into boiling soup. Simmer for 15–20 minutes.

Kubba Shells

INDIA   Tova Saul

Serves 4   Preparation 20 mins   Cook 35 mins   Advance   Freezable

Shells   *Filling*
2 cups ground rice   2 onions, grated and drained for 1 hour
8 oz minced meat (225 g)   8 oz minced meat (225 g)
Dash of pepper   Salt
¼ tsp salt   Pinch of turmeric
Water to mix

Filling: Mix all ingredients and reserve.
Shells: Mix the rice with the meat, pepper and salt and then add water gradually to make a smooth dough. Fill a saucer with water to wet your palms. Then divide the dough into balls (walnut size). Hollow out each piece of dough with your wet fingers, fill with ½ teaspoon of the filling and then pinch together firmly. Wet your palms again and roll each piece of dough to make an even, round ball. Drop the kubba into boiling soup and simmer gently for about 35 minutes. Serve in the soup. May also be served on their own with curries.

Meat Filled Kneidlach

LITHUANIA   Sally Bloom

Serves 8–10   Preparation 20 mins   Refrigerate 40 mins   Cook 40 mins

8 oz top rib beef cooked in chicken soup   *Kneidlach mixture*
   (225 g)   5–6 tbls medium matzo meal
1 tbls chicken fat   2 tbls chicken soup
1 onion, chopped   2 eggs, beaten
1 pint chicken soup (570 ml)   1 tsp salt
                                                  1 tsp pepper
                                                  2 tbls ground almonds
                                                  2 tbls chicken fat

Mix all the kneidlach ingredients together. Refrigerate for 40 minutes when the mixture should be firm enough to roll into soft balls. Mince the beef. Fry the mince with the onion in a little chicken fat. When cold, make the kneidlach mixture into balls and fill with small portions of the meat mixture. Drop the kneidlach into a pan of just boiling water. Cover and simmer for 40 minutes.

Matzo Balls

ENGLAND   Margaret Dent

Serves 4   **Preparation 10 mins**   **Cook 15 mins approx**

5 matzos
3 oz schmaltz (85 g)
2 eggs, beaten
Salt and pepper

2 small onions, finely chopped
Parsley, chopped
Marjoram, chopped

Crush the matzos in a large bowl. Add all other ingredients and beat well. Form into balls and boil in the soup for 10–15 minutes approximately. Do not use matzo meal in this recipe as it gives a floury taste.

Matzo Kleis

PORTUGAL   Joyce Keyes

Preparation 35 mins   **Resting time 30 mins**   **Cook 20 mins**

2 matzos
1 egg, beaten
2 tbls fine matzo meal

1 onion, chopped
Salt and pepper
Ginger to taste

Soak the matzos in cold water for ½ hour and squeeze dry. Sauté the onion until brown. Mix the matzos, onion, egg and seasonings well. Rest the mixture in the fridge for ½ hour. Roll into balls and then roll in fine matzo meal. Place in boiling soup 20 minutes before required and cook on a low heat.

This was traditionally served during Passover.

Potato Kliskelech

POLAND   Greta Goldwater

Serves 6   **Preparation 15 mins**   **Cook 30 mins**

5–6 large potatoes, grated
1 egg
Salt and pepper

1 medium onion, grated
Fine matzo meal to bind

Thoroughly strain liquid from onion and potato. Mix all ingredients with enough matzo meal to make a firm consistency – this is very important. Form the mixture into small balls. These must be very firm or they will disintegrate when boiling. Place the balls (smaller than kneidlach) into a saucepan of boiling water and allow to cook slowly for 20 to 30 minutes. Lift out and serve in chicken or split-pea soup.

Cold Apricot Soup

POLAND   Jane Finestone

Serves 5–6   **Preparation 10 mins**   **Cook 10 mins approx**

1 lb apricots (450 g)   1 oz sugar (30 g)
Pinch cinnamon   2 pints water (1.2 litres)
¼ cup sour cream

Boil apricots, sugar, cinnamon and water, stirring occasionally, until pulped. Remove from heat and sieve to get rid of stones. When cool, stir in sour cream (see page 217). Serve as cold as possible. The same recipe can be adapted to make apple or plum soup.

Bean and Farfel Soup

POLAND   Rebecca Bonstein

Serves 6   **Soaking time 4 hrs**   **Preparation 10 mins**   **Cook 1½ hrs approx**

1 lb haricot beans, soaked (or butter beans   2 tbls oil
    or mixture) (450 g)   3–4 carrots, sliced
1 medium Spanish onion, coarsely chopped   2 stalks of celery
½ large Spanish onion, chopped   Salt and pepper
2 pints beef stock (1.2 litres)   Small pasta shapes (optional)

Put beans, carrots, celery, beef stock and the half onion into a large saucepan of water and bring to the boil. Remove scum. Reduce heat and cook slowly, covered. Pour oil into a frying pan and fry remaining onion until very brown. Strain and add to the soup. Cook until beans are soft. Season. Cook small pasta shapes separately and add when serving soup if desired.

Green Bean Vichyssoise

CZECHOSLOVAKIA   Jackie Gryn

Serves 4–6   **Preparation 10 mins**   **Cook 30 mins approx**

1 lb green stringless beans (450 g)   1 pint cold milk (½ litre)
1 small carton sour cream   Juice of half a lemon or 1 tbls vinegar
Salt and pepper to taste   1 tbls flour

Break beans into 1" (2.5 cm) pieces. Cook in boiling salted water (barely covered) until *al dente*. Slake flour with 1 tablespoon cold milk and then add to beans and water with the remaining milk. Bring to the boil while stirring. Add the sour cream and lemon juice (or vinegar) and season to taste. As an alternative, cubed potatoes can be substituted for the beans.

Meat Beetroot Soup

LITHUANIA   Rusty Sotnick

Serves 10   **Preparation 20 mins**   **Cook 2½ hrs**

Soup
1 marrow bone
2 onions
Salt and pepper
4 pints water (2¼ litres)
3 lb raw beetroot with skin (1.3 kg)
1 tbls sugar
½ tbls acetic acid

Meat balls
1½ lb minced beef (675 g)
1 onion, chopped
1 egg, beaten
Salt and pepper

To serve
1 lb boiled new potatoes (450 g)

Cover the bone with the water, bring to the boil and skim. Add the onions and seasonings and cook for 2 hours. Strain and reserve stock. In a separate pan, boil the beetroot until soft enough to remove skin. When cool, skin and chop the beetroot finely. Mix the minced beef with onion, egg and seasonings and form into small balls. Heat the stock, add the meat balls and simmer for 30 minutes until cooked. Add the beetroot, acetic acid, sugar and salt and pepper to taste. Serve with boiled new potatoes.

Summer Borscht

AUSTRIA   Guggy Grahame

Serves 8   **Preparation 15 mins**   **Cook 1½–2 hrs**   **Advance**

2 lb raw beetroot (900 g)
2 pints water (1 litre)
Juice of 1½ lemons
3 tbls sugar

2 eggs
1 level tsp salt
Sour cream or sliced hard boiled egg

Peel and cut beetroot into smallish pieces, sprinkle with salt, cover with 2 pints cold water, bring to the boil and simmer until beetroot is soft. Remove beetroot but keep the liquid on the boil. Whisk eggs until frothy, add lemon juice and sugar, then pour the boiling liquid over the egg mixture, whisking all the time until well mixed. Taste for flavour and add more seasoning if necessary. Return beetroot to soup. Serve with 1 tablespoon of sour cream or sliced hard boiled egg.

Cold Buttermilk Soup

DENMARK   Birthe Tager

Serves 4   **Preparation 15 mins**   **Cook 10 mins**   **Advance**

Soup/drink
2 eggs
1½ oz sugar (40 g)
1 pint 12 fl oz buttermilk (910 ml)
Grated rind of 1 large lemon

Croûtons
2 slices white bread
1 oz sugar, optional (30 g)
2 oz butter (55 g)

Soup: Whisk the eggs and sugar together until well mixed and then add the buttermilk and grated rind and mix thoroughly.
Croûtons: Remove crusts from the bread and cut the slices into small squares and mix in the sugar if using it. Melt the butter in a frying pan and fry the bread squares until golden brown. Allow the croûtons to cool in the frying pan and serve with the soup.

Ferbrenter Soup – Burnt Soup

POLAND   Rebecca Bonstein

Serves 6   **Preparation 20 mins**   **Cook 1 hr**

4 large potatoes, sliced
1 tbls flour
2 tbls oil, for frying
1 medium Spanish onion, chopped
Salt and pepper

Dumplings
3 tbls plain flour
1 tsp chicken fat/maschick
Salt and pepper
Water to mix

Place potatoes in a pan and cover with water, add salt and bring to the boil. Reduce heat and cook slowly. In the meantime, fry the onion in a pan with the oil. When golden brown, add the flour, stirring continuously on the heat until the oil is absorbed. The onions will brown and the flour will begin to burn. Remove from hob and add to the potatoes and continue to cook slowly.
Dumplings: Mix the flour, salt and pepper and a teaspoonful of chicken fat or maschick and then add enough water to form a dough. Make into dumplings. Add to the soup and cook slowly for 45–60 minutes.

Cabbage Borscht

POLAND   Greta Goldwater

Serves 4   **Preparation 15 mins**   **Cook 2½ hours approx**   **Advance**   **Freezable**

2 lb white cabbage, shredded (450 g)
Salt and pepper
Lemon juice to taste
2 onions, chopped
Cinnamon

Handful of raisins
Handful of long grain rice
Sugar
Oil or chicken fat for frying

Sauté onions in chicken fat or oil in large saucepan until softened. At the same time, blanch the cabbage in boiling salted water for 4 minutes and then strain. Add cabbage to the onions and cover well with hot water. Add raisins, rice, cinnamon, lemon juice, sugar, salt and pepper. Cover and simmer for 2 hours, stirring occasionally.

Best Chicken Soup with Matzo Balls

FRANCE   Lady Jakobovits

Serves 8   **Preparation 30 mins**   **Cook 2¾ hrs**   **Refrigerate overnight**

4 lb boiling fowl and giblets (1.8 kg)
3 leeks, thickly sliced
3 carrots, sliced
2 whole onions
Salt and pepper
Pinch of sugar
2 glasses beef gravy

Matzo balls
2 large eggs, beaten
6 tsp soft margarine
1 tsp salt
4–5 oz fine matzo meal (115–140 g)

Soup: Place fowl and giblets in your oldest and most frequently used pot. Cover with water and bring to the boil. Remove scum and add leeks, carrots and onions and bring back to the boil. Cover and simmer until chicken is tender. Allow to cool and refrigerate overnight. Remove fat and vegetables, season with salt, pepper and a pinch of sugar and add the gravy. Boil again, add matzo balls, cover and allow them to simmer for approximately 20 minutes.

Matzo balls: Mix all ingredients to a light consistency and refrigerate for 30 minutes. With wet hands, roll into small balls. This mixture should make approximately 10 balls.

This recipe was made in an old stone pot and traditionally served on Friday night.

Murug – Indian Chicken Soup

INDIA   Mavis Hyman

Serves 6–8   **Preparation 10 mins**   **Cook 1 hr**

5 lb roasting chicken, portioned and
   skinned (2.25 kg)
1 small onion, sliced
1 clove garlic, crushed
10 fl oz cold water (285 ml)

Salt and pepper to taste
1 tsp fresh ginger, grated
1 tbls vegetable oil
1 tsp turmeric powder
1 cardamom pod

In a deep saucepan stirfry onion, garlic and ginger in the oil. When onion is transparent add turmeric, cardamom, salt, pepper and water. Bring to the boil and cook until liquid has reduced a little. Add chicken pieces and bring to boil over a high heat. Stir thoroughly and cook for 15 minutes, until juices are absorbed into the chicken. Add 2½ pints (1¼ litres) cold water and simmer until chicken is tender (approximately 45 minutes). If desired, potatoes can be added with this water. Serve hot with boiled rice.

Dal Soup

INDIA   Mavis Hyman

Serves 4   **Preparation 5 mins**   **Cook 30 mins approx**

1 cup red lentils, washed
1 cup boiling water
2 tsp cumin powder
1 tsp salt

1 small onion, sliced
½ cup cold water
2 cloves garlic, grated
2 tbls vegetable oil

Place lentils in saucepan and cover with the cup of boiling water and keep on the boil. Add onion and simmer until lentils are soft (approximately 15 minutes), stirring frequently to ensure that the water is absorbed. Add enough cold water to make a smooth consistency. Continue to simmer. Meanwhile heat cumin powder, garlic, salt and oil in a small pan over a moderate heat. When oil begins to smoke, add this mixture gradually to the lentils, taking great care as the oil will bubble when added. Stir vigorously, then add more salt to taste. Serve hot with boiled rice.

Goldzip – Golden Soup

HUNGARY

Serves 10–12   Preparation 10 mins   Cook 3 hrs   Refrigerate overnight   Freezable

1 large boiling fowl, halved
4 medium carrots
1 tbls salt
1 tsp saffron shreds

3–4 parsley roots or parsnips
1 medium onion
7–8 black peppercorns
5 pints water (3 litres)

Place the fowl in a large saucepan, cover with the water and bring to the boil over a medium heat. Skim, add the vegetables, salt and pepper and then simmer for at least 2½ hours. Add the saffron just before the soup is ready and stir in well. Strain the soup and refrigerate overnight. Remove fat.

This soup was traditionally served at weddings and was accompanied by finger noodles.

Goulash Soup

AUSTRIA   Ruth Smilg

Serves 6–8   Preparation 10 mins   Cook 35–40 mins   Advance

3 large onions
Fat for frying
1 tbls paprika
1 tsp salt
Caraway seeds to taste

½ lb beef, cubed (225 g)
1 tbls tomato purée
3 large potatoes, cubed
Dash of vinegar

Slice onions finely, fry in fat until golden brown, add paprika, salt, caraway seeds and vinegar. Add meat, stir once and then add tomato purée. Continue stirring until nicely browned, then add water to cover. Simmer, covered, very slowly for 20 minutes, then add potatoes. Simmer until potatoes are soft. Adjust seasonings and add a little water if necessary.

Lemon Soup

ROMANIA   Hermy Jankel

Serves 4–6   Preparation 5 mins   Cook 15 mins

2 pints *cold* chicken soup (1.15 litres)
2 beaten egg yolks
1 cup cooked rice

Juice of 2 lemons
2 tbls sugar
Chopped dill to taste

Add the lemon juice to cold chicken soup, heat slowly and pour a little onto beaten egg yolks, stirring continuously. When well mixed pour egg mixture back into the saucepan still stirring – do not allow to boil. Add sugar and cooked rice and keep hot. Do not boil. Add chopped dill for an interesting taste and serve.

Lentil Soup

GERMANY   Minnie Nedas

Serves 6–8   **Soak overnight**   **Preparation 20 mins**   **Cook 2½ hrs**

2 cups lentils or split peas
1 marrow bone
1 lb brisket (450 g)
2 carrots
2 sticks celery, diced

2 quarts water (2¼ litres)
2 tsp salt
1 onion, diced
2 frankfurters
Pepper to taste

Cover dried pulses with water and soak overnight. Drain. Place bone in water with meat, salt and pepper, bring to the boil, reduce heat, and simmer for 1 hour. Skim, add lentils and vegetables and simmer until cooked (1½ hours). Remove meat and bone. Strain. Sieve lentils and add with diced frankfurters to stock and reheat. You can use lima beans instead of lentils, when you then add 2 potatoes and ¾ cup of pearl barley.

Linzensoep – Dutch Lentil Soup

HOLLAND   Nanny ten Brink-de-Lieme

Serves 10   **Preparation 10 mins**   **Cook 2 hrs**   **Advance**   **Freezable**

5 pints beef stock (3 litres)
Salt
1 lb wurst sausage (450 g)
3½ oz margarine (100 g)

14 oz brown lentils (400 g)
2 onions, finely chopped
1 bay leaf
1 tbls flour

Sauté the onions in the margarine. Cook lentils in the stock with onions and bay leaf for about 2 hours. Slice the wurst and add to the soup for the last half hour of cooking time. Add salt to taste. To thicken soup, if necessary, mix 1 tablespoon of flour with a little cold water and stir into the soup. Serve with slices of the wurst in the soup, or handed separately, with bread.

Meat Soup

CZECHOSLOVAKIA Ruth Arnold

Serves 10–12 **Preparation 20 mins** **Cook 6 hrs approx**

4½ lb lean beef (2 kg)
2 pigeons
1 breast of goose
Salt and pepper

1 piece of liver
1 boiling fowl
Assorted vegetables: turnips, leeks, carrots,
    onions, etc.

Place all the ingredients in a pan. Cover with water and bring to the boil. Skim and then simmer on a low heat for several hours. When ready, sieve. To serve, add lockshen or rice plus the yolk of an egg to make it richer.

This recipe is taken from a cookery book dated 1918 and was in use before the Second World War.

Split Pea Soup I

POLAND Greta Goldwater

Serves 6–8 **Preparation 15 mins** **Cook 1 hr**

8 oz split peas (225 g)
1 onion, chopped
2 carrots, sliced
2 leeks, sliced
Handful chopped parsley
1 turnip, chopped

½ swede, chopped
1 parsnip, sliced
1 potato, sliced
Salt and pepper
Oil for frying

Fry onion until soft. Add all other ingredients and cover with water. Cook on a low heat for 1 hour. This is nice served with potato kliskelech (see page 81).

Split Pea Soup II

RUSSIA Frances Ravden

Serves 4–6 **Soaking time 1 hr** **Preparation 10 mins** **Cook 3 hrs**

Knuckle of veal or chicken giblets
1 onion, chopped
4 oz split peas (115 g)
Salt and pepper

2 carrots, chopped
1 turnip, chopped
2 potatoes, peeled

Soak split peas. Put knuckle of veal (or giblets) in a saucepan and cover well with water. Bring to the boil and skim. Add the carrots, onion, turnip and split peas. Cut up potatoes and add to soup. Simmer, covered, for 3 hours. If desired, meat balls or kneidlach may be added.

Pumpkin Soup I

MOROCCO   Esther Bloomberg

Serves 8   Soaking time 12 hrs   Preparation 30 mins   Cook 1 hr   Advance

4 pints stock (beef or chicken) (2¼ litres)   2 lb pumpkin, peeled and chopped (900 g)
8 oz chickpeas (225 g)   1 tbls sugar
2 medium onions, chopped   Salt and pepper

Although the original recipe calls for stock made with marrow bones and beef, you can substitute leaner bones or even stock cubes. Soak chickpeas overnight, then drain and remove the peel. Add the onions and chickpeas to the stock, bring to the boil and simmer for 30 minutes, then add pumpkin and sugar and cook for a further 20 minutes. Add salt and pepper to taste, put through a blender and reheat, until soup is of a fairly thick consistency.

Pumpkin Soup II

AUSTRALIA   Elana Schlesinger

Serves 6   Preparation 10 mins   Cook 30 mins   Advance

1 lb 12 oz pumpkin, peeled (750 g)   2 vegetable/chicken stock cubes
2 oz butter or margarine (60 g)   1 tsp salt
2 cups boiling water   ½ cup cream (optional)
½ tsp pepper   *Garnish*
3 onions, chopped   Chopped chives

Cut pumpkin into wedges and cook in unsalted water until tender. Drain and cool. Fry the onions gently in butter until soft but not brown. Purée the pumpkin, onion, stock cubes, water, salt and pepper until smooth. Reheat and just before serving stir in cream (if desired) and garnish with chopped chives.

Sauerkraut Vichyssoise

CZECHOSLOVAKIA   Jackie Gryn

Serves 6   Preparation 5 mins   Cook 30 mins

2 tins kidney beans, drained   1 jar sauerkraut, rinsed
1 pint milk (½ litre)   1 small carton sour cream
1 tbls flour   Salt and pepper to taste
1 pint water (½ litre)

Place the beans and the sauerkraut in a saucepan and cover with water. Slake the flour in a tablespoon of the milk and add to the pan with the remaining milk, stirring until it boils. Add the sour cream and seasonings and cook for approximately 30 minutes.

Stufe Borscht – Sorrel Soup

POLAND   Greta Goldwater

Serves 4   **Preparation 15 mins**   **Cook 25 mins**   **Advance**

1 lb sorrel (450 g)   1½ pints water (1 litre)
5 tbls lemon juice   2 eggs
Salt and pepper   Sour cream (optional)

Wash the sorrel well and chop the leaves. Place leaves in salted water with lemon juice. Season with salt and pepper. Cover and simmer until soft. Remove from heat. Beat eggs in a bowl and then add a little soup to them, mixing well. Stir egg mixture into soup and heat gently, allowing the eggs to thicken the soup. Do not boil as the eggs will curdle. Serve hot or cold as desired. Before serving add sour cream if wished.

Cold Summer Soup

EGYPT   Doris Afif

Serves 6   **Preparation 10 mins**   **Cook 20 mins**   **Refrigerate 3 hrs**   **Advance**

3½ pints goat's milk (2 litres)   6 large eggs
1 lb small courgettes, sliced and parboiled   2 tsp dried mint
   (450 g)   *Garnish*
Salt and pepper to taste   Croûtons

Gently boil the milk on a low heat and add the courgettes, allowing them to cook thoroughly. Gently break eggs into milk, allowing them to poach one at a time. Remove eggs when cooked. When milk comes up to first boil add salt and pepper to taste and dried mint. Leave to cool and then refrigerate. Serve cold from the fridge, adding the poached eggs and croûtons.

Tomato Soup

ROMANIA   Charlotte Davis

Serves 10   **Preparation 15 mins**   **Cook 35 mins approx**   **Advance**   **Freezable**

12 lb tomatoes, skinned (5.45 kg)   3 bay leaves
2 large onions, sliced   Salt
Freshly ground black pepper   Butter/vegetable oil

Sauté the onions in a little oil or butter and then add tomatoes, bay leaves, salt and pepper. Mix thoroughly. Cover and simmer, stirring occasionally, until tomatoes have softened. Mash to a pulp and then allow to cook for another 2–3 minutes. Remove from heat and take out bay leaves. Sieve the soup – do not use liquidiser. Adjust seasonings and serve hot.

Heimesha Water Soup

POLAND   Renee Linder

Serves 4   **Preparation 10 mins**   **Cook 45 mins**

1 large Spanish onion, chopped
2 tbls cooked farfel
Salt and pepper
1½ pints water (1 litre)

3 tbls peas
½ tsp marmite (optional)
1 tbls chicken fat or margarine
Diced cooked potato (optional)

Fry onion in the fat until golden brown. Transfer to a saucepan, add boiling water and all other ingredients except for the farfel and cook for 45 minutes on a gentle simmer. If desired, a small amount of diced potato can be added to thicken soup. Add farfel just before serving.

FISH

Bhetki Fish

INDIA

Serves 4–6 **Preparation 5 mins** **Standing time 1 hr** **Gas No 8, 450°F, 230°C**
Cook 10 mins approx

2 lb thick fillet of flounder (900 g)
2 tbls coriander powder
2 tbls cumin powder
¼ tsp cayenne or 1 small green chilli, finely
   blended

1 tsp salt
½ tsp turmeric
1½ tsp oil
2 tbls lemon juice
2 tsp yoghurt (optional)

Roast together in a hot, dry small pan the coriander and cumin powders. Add turmeric, cayenne or chilli, lemon juice, oil and salt and mix to a paste. Stir in yoghurt if desired. Rub on fish and leave for 1 hour. Bake, uncovered, in an oven for 10 minutes or until fish flesh is opaque.

Ala Alas – Stuffed Carp

YUGOSLAVIA Bulka Danon

Serves 8 **Preparation 20 mins** **Cook 20 mins** **Gas No 6, 400°F, 200°C**

4 lb 4 oz carp (2 kg)
3 large onions, chopped
1 lb 10 oz carrots, grated (750 g)
Generous handful chopped parsley

Salt and black pepper
Flour to coat
Sunflower oil

Filling: Fry the onions and carrots in a little oil. When nearly soft, add parsley, salt and pepper to taste.
Clean the carp, dry and coat in flour. Fry lightly in oil. Drain the carp and use half the filling to stuff the cavity. Place the fish in a baking dish and cover with the rest of the filling. Bake. Serve hot with boiled potatoes or rice.

This recipe was often served at the start of Shabbat.

Boiled Stuffed Carp I

POLAND   Guggy Grahame

Serves 5–6   **Preparation 20 mins**   **Cook 25–30 mins**   **Advance**

3 lb carp, sliced (1.4 kg)

Stuffing
Tail of the carp, skinned and filleted
2 fresh herrings, skinned and filleted
6 oz fresh haddock, skinned and filleted
  (170 g)
1 small onion
1 tbls ground almonds
1 dsp fine matzo meal
1 egg, lightly beaten
1 tsp sugar
Salt and pepper

Stock
2 pints cold water (1.2 litres)
1 lb onions, sliced (450 g)
2 medium carrots, sliced
1 stalk celery, chopped
Small bunch parsley and dill, tied together
2 tsp sugar
½ tsp pepper
1 tsp salt

Stock: Place all stock ingredients in a large pan and bring to the boil, simmer for 15 minutes and reserve.

Stuffing: Mince the tail of the carp, herrings, haddock and onion. Add all other stuffing ingredients and mix well. Stuff spaces in the fish and the head of the carp, but not too full as the mixture expands when boiled.

Place fish pieces on the vegetables in the stock so that they do not touch each other. Simmer the fish for about 25–30 minutes. Taste the liquid and add more seasoning if desired. Leave to cool in the pan and then carefully lift out fish slices, put them into a dish and strain the clear liquid over them. This will form a jelly as it cools. Decorate with carrot slices.

Stuffed Carp II

POLAND
Esther Eisen

Serves 6–7   Preparation 30 mins   Cook 1¼ hrs   Advance

3lb carp (1.4 kg)

Stuffing
2 lb minced fish, including bream (900 g)
4 eggs, beaten
Salt, pepper and sugar to taste
2 medium onions, chopped
2 tbls matzo meal

Stock
5 carrots, sliced
2 large onions, sliced
Salt, pepper and sugar to taste

Remove head of carp. Do not slit belly as the innards must be removed after slicing fish so that a complete circle of fish can be filled. Cut fish into six or seven slices. Mix together all stuffing ingredients. Fill the cavity of each slice of fish with the stuffing and flatten with knife. Prepare the stock in a saucepan, allowing enough water with the sliced onion and carrots to cover the fish. Bring to the boil, then place fish carefully in saucepan. Cover and simmer gently, adding salt, pepper and sugar to taste. The liquid will reduce in cooking. Carp head should be used in cooking as it will add to the flavour.

Carp in Jelly

AUSTRIA
Ruth Smilg

Serves 6 approx   Preparation 15 mins   Cook 45 mins   Advance

4–5 lb carp (2–2.2 kg)
2 carrots
A few peppercorns
Salt
2 tbls wine vinegar
1 onion
1 stick celery

1 bay leaf
1 tbls lemon juice
Pinch thyme
Potatoes (optional)
Garnish
Chopped pickled cucumbers

Wash, clean and scale carp, remove head and cut fish into pieces 1" (2.5 cm) wide. Cut onion, carrots and celery into strips and cook in salted water until tender. Strain liquid into another saucepan, set aside cooked vegetables. Make up the liquid to 2 pints (1¼ litres), add a few peppercorns, bay leaf, salt, lemon juice, thyme and vinegar and simmer for 20 minutes. Add the carp pieces and head, and simmer, covered, until fish is cooked – about 12 to 15 minutes. Lift out fish carefully and arrange in a deep dish. Arrange the cooked vegetables around the fish, adding a few chopped pickled cucumbers. Reduce stock in which the fish was cooked to half by cooking briskly in an open pan, adjust seasoning, adding a little more vinegar if necessary, then strain liquid over fish. Leave to set. Potatoes can be cooked in the stock and arranged with the other vegetables if desired.

Marinated Jellied Carp

RUSSIA   Guggy Grahame

Serves 6   **Preparation 20 mins**   **Cook 1 hr**   **Refrigerate 24 hrs**   **Advance**

3½ lb carp (1½ kg)
1 lemon, sliced
12 cloves
6 bay leaves
Head and tail of carp

Marinade
1½ lb onions, thinly sliced (675 g)
1 pint cold water (½ litre)
3 tbls acetic acid
2 tbls sugar

Boil all marinade ingredients together until onions are soft. Strain and put the clear liquid on a low heat in a large, wide pan. Clean and slice the carp, leaving the skin on. Put the slices into the prepared marinade so that the pieces do not touch one another. Bring to the boil, skim, then reduce the heat and simmer for about 15 minutes. Taste and adjust flavour – it has to be sweet and sour. As the fish boils, the liquid may reduce – add more water, if necessary, so that the fish is always covered. Carefully remove the fish without breaking and place in an oblong pyrex dish. Put thin slices of lemon on each piece of fish. When all the fish has been removed, taste the liquid again and make sure it is to your liking, and pour over enough to cover all the fish. Drop 12 cloves and 6 bay leaves into the dish, cover with clingfilm or foil and refrigerate for at least 24 hours, and up to 3 days, before serving. Serve as an hors d'œuvre with melba toast or as a main course.

Hot Fish Balls

MOROCCO   Esther Bloomberg

Serves 3–4   **Preparation 20 mins**   **Cook 20 mins approx**

1 lb of white fish – hake, cod or haddock,
    filleted (450 g)
½ cup medium matzo meal
1 egg, beaten
Rind of ¾ lemon, finely grated
Juice of half a lemon

1–2 tbls parsley, chopped
½ tsp salt
Pepper to taste
4 tbls oil
10 fl oz water (285 ml)

Mash fish roughly with a fork or put through a food processor if you prefer a smoother texture, add a good half cup of matzo meal (or cholla soaked in water for a few minutes and drained). If matzo meal is used add the same quantity of boiling water. Mix well. Add the egg, lemon rind, parsley, salt and a little pepper. Mix thoroughly. Form fish balls with hands or 2 oiled spoons. Put water and oil in a saucepan and bring to boil. Simmer fish balls for 15 minutes then add lemon juice and simmer for 5 more minutes. Serve.

Gefilte Fish Balls I

ENGLAND   Zoe Josephs

Serves 3–4   **Preparation 15 mins**   **Cook 15 mins**

1 lb fish, chopped (450 g)
1 large onion, grated
1 apple, grated
2 eggs, lightly beaten
Acetic acid to taste

1 dsp parsley, chopped
Pinch of ginger
Sugar to taste
Salt and pepper
Flour or matzo meal for coating

Mix all the ingredients except one of the eggs together and form into balls. Roll in flour or matzo meal. Dip in seasoned egg, then fry in deep oil until brown. These balls can also be boiled in fish stock with onion, carrots, peppercorns, bay leaf and salt.

Gefilte Fish Balls II

RUSSIA   Jennifer Melman

Serves 3   **Preparation 10 mins**   **Cook 1 hr 20 mins**

1 lb mixed white fish, minced (450 g)
2 tbls fine matzo meal
1 egg, beaten
¼ glass cold water
Salt and pepper

Stock
Skin and bones of fish
1 large carrot, sliced
Salt and pepper
Garnish
Carrot slices

Stock: Place the skin and bones of the fish in a large pan. Cover with water and bring to the boil. Remove any scum, add the rest of the stock ingredients and simmer for 20 minutes. Strain.
Fish balls: Mix all the ingredients together to a consistency which can be easily rolled into loose balls. Gently poach fish balls with the carrot slices in the stock, covered, for about 1 hour. Decorate each fish ball with a slice of carrot on top and serve cold with a little stock poured over and accompanied by chrane.

Fish On A Green Sauce

FRANCE   Odette Dreyfuss

Serves 4   **Preparation 15 mins**   **Cook 40 mins approx**

4 slices of pike or 4 whole trout   1½ tbls oil
1 large onion, finely chopped   1 tbls flour
2 garlic cloves, finely chopped   Salt and pepper
Generous handful of parsley, minced   10 fl oz water (285 ml)

Heat oil in pan large enough to hold the quantity of fish. Add onion and garlic and fry until slightly golden. Add the parsley. Make a sauce by adding flour, salt and pepper to the pan and slowly adding the water, stirring until sauce has the right consistency. Add fish to pan. According to thickness of fish, cook for 20–30 minutes (do not overcook) and then place pieces of fish on a flat dish and pour the sauce over. Serve either hot or cold.

Fish Khutta

INDIA   Mavis Hyman

Serves 4   **Preparation 10 mins**   **Cook 15 mins**

1 onion, chopped   1½ pints (1 litre) cold water
A little oil   1 tsp salt
1 tsp fresh ginger, grated   Pinch of turmeric
½ tsp garlic, grated   Pepper to taste
1 tbls fresh mint, chopped   Small pieces of fried fish
1 tsp sugar   Juice of 1 lemon

Glaze the onions in a little vegetable oil in a saucepan with the ginger, garlic, turmeric, salt and pepper. Add 1½ pints (1 litre) cold water and bring to the boil. Add pieces of fish which have already been fried until golden brown, and simmer for 10 minutes. Add the mint, lemon juice and sugar and simmer for a further 5 minutes. Serve hot.

Fish in Lemon Jelly

AUSTRIA   Ilse Schwarzmann

Serves 8   **Preparation 30 mins**   **Cook 45 mins**   **Advance**

8 slices fish   2 medium onions, sliced
Salt   2 peppercorns
Lemon juice to taste   1 packet lemon jelly
1 dsp vinegar   2 dsp sugar
1 bay leaf

Wash fish, season with salt and allow to stand for a while. Boil onions in enough water to cover the fish. Place fish in the boiling water, then add vinegar and sugar and boil for about 30 minutes. Add peppercorns, bay leaf and jelly and as much lemon juice as desired, boil for a few minutes. Remove from stove, put fish into a dish with the strained liquid, cool and then place in refrigerator to set.

Caramelised Herrings

ROMANIA/HUNGARY   Ignatz Rub

Serves 2   **Preparation 5 mins**   **Soaking time 2 hrs**   **Cook 35 mins**

3 schmaltz herrings, soaked   1 onion, sliced in rings
1½ tbls sugar

When herrings have been soaked, slice them thickly. Place sugar in a saucepan and heat gently until it begins to colour. Add a little hot water. Place onions in the pan and bring to the boil. Cover and allow to cook for 10 minutes. Then add the fish and continue cooking, covered, for a further 20 minutes.

Red Mullet with Pine Kernels and Raisins

ITALY   Celeste Zarfati

Serves 4   **Preparation 10 mins**   **Cook 30 mins approx**

8 red mullet   1 large glass vinegar
1½ oz pine kernels (45 g)   Salt and pepper
Handful of raisins   Olive oil

Put the cleaned fish into a large pan, head by tail alternately. Dribble olive oil over them, then add all other ingredients. Cook for about 30 minutes, simmering gently. Do not touch the fish during cooking. Serve cold.

This dish was often used by my grandmother, Miriam di Veroli, in celebration of Rosh Hashana.

Peshe El Salsa – Marinated Fish

SALONIKA/GREECE   Flory Raychbart

Serves 4   Preparation 15 mins   Cook 15 mins   Marinate 2–3 days   Advance

2½ lb bream fillets (1.1 kg)
1 level tsp paprika
3 tbls vinegar
Corn oil

4 oz ground walnuts (115 g)
Salt and black pepper
1 tbls breadcrumbs or medium matzo meal

Slice the fillets into 2″ (5 cm) pieces. Fry them in a little corn oil until cooked through. Remove them and reserve.

Sauce: Place 2 tablespoons of oil in frying pan and heat gently. Add the walnuts with breadcrumbs or matzo meal. Add seasonings and continue to heat, stirring until mixture becomes light brown. Add vinegar and bring to the boil. Turn down heat and allow to simmer for 2–3 minutes, still stirring. If mixture is too dry, add a little more vinegar and water.

Place the fish in a dish and cover with the sauce – there should be sufficient liquid to cover fish completely; if not, make some more sauce. Cover the dish and leave in fridge for 2–3 days. Serve cold.

Pike Stuffed with Walnuts

HUNGARY

**Serves 4   Preparation 10 mins   Salting time 1 hr   Gas No 4, 350°F, 180°C
Cook 30 mins approx**

2.2 lb pike (1 kg)
7 oz walnuts, coarsely chopped (200 g)
Salt and ground black pepper

2 slices cholla
2 egg yolks

Clean the fish and sprinkle with salt and leave for 1 hour. Soak the cholla in water and squeeze dry. Add the egg yolks, salt and pepper to the cholla and mix together with the walnuts. Place the nut mixture into the cavity of the pike and sew up. Place the fish in a greased ovenproof dish and cover with buttered foil. Bake.

Salmon Patties

AUSTRALIA   Goldie Selig

Serves 6   **Preparation 10 mins**   **Cook 40 mins to 1 hr**

1 lb 12 oz tinned red salmon (800 g)   Breadcrumbs
2 medium potatoes, boiled   Plain flour
Lemon juice   Frying oil
Parsley, chopped   *Garnish*
Salt and pepper   Lemon wedges
2 eggs

Mash potatoes, mix with the well-drained salmon and season to taste with salt, pepper, lemon juice and parsley. Add the eggs and if necessary enough breadcrumbs to make a good consistency. Form into dessertspoon-size balls and roll in plain flour. Deep fry. Drain well and serve with lemon wedges.

These salmon patties were served with mashed potatoes and peas cooked with mint. (In the 1930s vegetables were often prepared and cooked an hour before they were brought to the table, so for a genuine result cook your peas until they are hard!) Made in a smaller size they were also served with cocktails and then they were garnished with multi-coloured pickling onions and an army of toothpicks.

Iraqi Salona

IRAQ

Serves 6–8   **Salting time 30 mins**   **Preparation 35 mins**   **Gas No 4, 350°F, 185°C**
                                                                         Cook 30 mins

3 lb haddock or fish of your   2 tbls parsley, finely chopped
  choice (1.3 kg)   Curry powder (optional)
1 green pepper, sliced   Salt
2 aubergines, peeled in alternate strips   *Sauce*
4 large onions, sliced   1 cup lemon juice
2 tomatoes, sliced   6 tbls sugar
5 tbls oil   Tomato paste
                                              Salt

Slice the aubergines and sprinkle with salt. Let them stand for half an hour in a sieve. Clean and salt the fish. Cut into serving slices and place in a greased ovenproof dish. Fry the aubergines, then the onions and sauté the green pepper. Sprinkle the fish with curry powder, if used, and add onions, green pepper and aubergines. Place the sliced tomatoes on top and sprinkle with parsley.

Mix all the ingredients for the sauce in a small saucepan and cook until slightly thickened. Pour over the fish and vegetables. Cover with foil and place in a moderate oven. Remove the foil after about 15 minutes. Taste the sauce and adjust seasoning. Replace the dish in the oven without the foil until most of the sauce has evaporated and the fish is cooked.

Note: The fish for the Salona can be fried. You can also omit the aubergines.

Talpechal

INDIA   Mavis Hyman

Serves 4–6   **Preparation 15 mins**   **Cook 30 mins approx**

2 lb white fish, filleted (900 g)
1 large onion, grated
3 cloves garlic, grated
½ tsp fresh root ginger, grated
4 oz fresh tomatoes, chopped (115 g)
   or 2 oz tomato purée (55 g)

3 tbls coconut or vegetable oil
1 oz fresh or dried curry leaves (30 g)
1 tsp coriander powder
1½ pints cold water (1 litre)
Vinegar, salt and pepper to taste

Sauté onion, garlic and ginger in the oil. When onions are glazed add curry leaves, coriander and tomatoes (or tomato purée). Stir until tomatoes are cooked through. Add cold water and bring to the boil. Add fish and boil again. Then simmer until the fish has been cooked through. Add vinegar, salt and pepper to taste.

This recipe was used by the Jews of Cochin.

MEAT

Beef

Roast Brisket

CANADA   Betty Crystal

Serves 8–10   **Preparation 10 mins**   **Gas No 3, 325°F, 180°C**   **Cook 2–3 hrs**

5 lb brisket (2¼ kg)
2 large onions, chopped
2 cloves garlic, chopped

Salt, pepper, paprika and
  dry mustard for seasoning
Oil for frying
Packet of dried onion soup (optional)

Fry the onions and garlic lightly in the oil and place in the bottom of a shallow roasting pan. Season brisket well and place on top of the onions. If desired, add the dried onion soup, then cover the bottom of the pan with hot water. Cover with foil and roast. This is better made the day before so that the fat can be removed from the gravy.

Chulent

POLAND   Esther Eisen

Serves 6–8   **Preparation 15 mins**   **Gas No ¼, 250°F, 120°C**   **Cook 18 hrs approx**

Handful barley
Handful haricot beans (soaked for 2 hrs)
Marrow bone

1 large onion, sliced
3½ lb piece fatty topside (1.5 kg)
Salt and pepper to taste

Place all ingredients in a saucepan and cover with water. Bring to the boil and skim and then boil for 5 minutes. Transfer to a heavy casserole dish and cook overnight in the oven on a low heat.

Grandma's Chulent with Potato Dumplings

POLAND   Greta Goldwater

Serves 4–6   Preparation 20 mins   Gas No ¼, 250°F, 120°C   Cook 18 hrs approx

Chulent
2½ lb brisket, in large slices (1.1 kg)
1 onion, chopped
1 marrow bone
8 oz butterbeans, soaked overnight (225 g)
2 lb potatoes (900 g)
Salt and pepper

Dumplings
1 lb potatoes, grated (450 g)
1 onion, grated
Fine matzo meal
Salt and pepper
Nutmeg

Put chopped onion in a heavy-bottomed casserole pan and place marrow bone on top. Add layers of meat, beans and potatoes. Combine all dumpling ingredients with enough matzo meal to make a very firm consistency. Form into dumplings and place them on top of the meat in the casserole. Cover well with stock or water. Bring to the boil and then cook overnight in a very low oven. Extra meat fat was often added to this recipe.

Chulent with Kugel

CZECHOSLOVAKIA   Jackie Gryn

**Serves 4–6   Soaking time 12 hrs   Preparation 15 mins   Gas No 1, 275°F, 150°C
Cook 24 hrs**

Chulent
1 lb red kidney beans (450 g)
2 oz medium pearl barley, rinsed (55 g)
1 tbls flour
1 tbls chicken fat or fat from chicken soup
2 cloves garlic
1 medium onion, chopped
8 oz flank of beef (flanken), cubed (225 g)
Salt and pepper
Paprika
6 eggs, pricked

Kugel
2 eggs
8 tbls flour
2 tbls chicken fat
1 small onion, chopped
Salt and pepper
Paprika

Chulent: Soak the beans overnight and rinse them the following morning. Add to the barley in an oven-to-table casserole and cover both with water and bring to the boil. Stir in the flour slaked in 1 tablespoon of water. Then add chicken fat, garlic, onion, seasonings and beef and bring to the boil. Lay eggs on top of the other ingredients and place covered casserole in oven for 24 hours. After 4 to 5 hours, remove eggs and shell them and chop with chicken fat. Serve separately or add to cooked chicken livers to make chopped liver.
Kugel: Work ingredients together and lay on top of chulent ingredients after removing the eggs. Replace cover on casserole and continue cooking.

Dfeena

EGYPT

Serves 4–6   **Preparation 15 mins**   **Gas No 4, 350°F, 185°C**   **Cook 16 hrs**

2 lb lean stewing beef, cubed (900 g)
1 calf's foot
6 small potatoes, peeled
6 eggs in their shells
2 large onions, finely chopped

8 oz chickpeas, soaked overnight (225 g)
2 cloves garlic, crushed
1 tsp ground allspice
Salt and pepper
Oil for frying

Blanch the calf's foot in boiling water. Fry the onions in oil until soft. Place the calf's foot, eggs and onions in a large casserole together with the drained chickpeas and all other ingredients. Cover with water and add the garlic and seasonings. Cover the pot and bake in the oven on Gas 4, 350°F, 185°C for 1 hour then reduce the temperature to the lowest possible heat and cook overnight.

Traditionally served as Shabbat lunch.

Do Piazcha – Two Onions

RUSSIA   Rosa Pine

Serves 4   **Preparation 20 mins**   **Cook 35–40 mins**

2 Spanish onions, finely chopped
1½ lb beef, cut into thin strips (675 g)
1½ lb ripe tomatoes, chopped (675 g)
Salt and pepper

2 cups water
3 tbls oil
Matzos

Fry onions in the oil until golden brown, add beef and cook for 15 minutes. Then add water and seasonings and cook slowly for 10 minutes. Add the tomatoes and continue to cook slowly until the water has evaporated and meat is tender. Serve immediately on matzos. Chips were usually served with this meal.

Goulash

HUNGARY　　　　　　　　　　　　　　　　　　　　　　　　Tania Slowe

Serves 4–6　Preparation 15 mins　Gas No 3, 325°F, 180°C　Cook 2–2½ hrs　Advance

2 lb stewing steak,
　trimmed and cubed (900 g)
2 medium onions, chopped
Vegetable oil for frying
1½ tbls sweet paprika
1 green pepper, sliced

1 × 14 oz tin of tomatoes (400 g)
½ tsp caraway seeds
1 lb potatoes, peeled (450 g)
Salt and pepper
1 glass red wine (optional)

Fry the onion and green pepper together over a medium heat until the onion is golden. Remove from heat and add paprika and ½ teaspoon salt and mix well. Add the meat to pan and fry for a few minutes until browned. Then add the tin of tomatoes (broken up) and the red wine if used. Add a little water if necessary (there must be sufficient liquid to cover the meat). Stir in caraway seeds and some freshly ground black pepper. Cook covered, in a medium oven for approximately 2 hours, or until the meat is really tender. About 20 minutes before the end of cooking time add the potatoes cut into small cubes, making sure again that there is enough liquid. Taste for seasoning and serve in soup bowls, as this is meant to be a hearty peasant stew.

Lubia – Libyan Chulent

LIBYA　　　　　　　　　　　　　　　　　　　　　　　　Eveleen Habib

Serves 4　　　　　　　　Preparation 15 mins　　　　　　　Cook 2–3 hrs approx

8 oz white haricot beans (225 g)
2 lb best stewing steak (900 g)
3 onions, grated
Salt and pepper
Cinnamon to taste

4 uncooked eggs in shells
2–3 tbls tomato purée
3–4 garlic cloves, crushed
4 medium potatoes, thickly sliced
Oil for frying

Put some oil in a heavy-bottomed saucepan and gently fry onions and garlic. Add beans, meat, tomato purée, seasonings and eggs (the latter will absorb all the colour and flavour of the food). Cover with water and once it has come to the boil, let it simmer slowly on top of the cooker. Add potatoes an hour before the end of the cooking stage. Just before serving, shell the eggs which can then be served separately or eaten with the stew. Serve with couscous.

The couscous is traditionally eaten cold by Libyan Jews, but other North African communities eat it hot.

Male Ptacci – Little Birds

CZECHOSLOVAKIA　　　　　　　　　　　　　　　　　　Hana Rayner

Serves 4　　　**Preparation 15 mins**　　　**Gas No 4, 350°F, 185°C**　　　**Cook 1¾ hrs**

4 silverside of beef fillets, beaten until quite
　thin
4 small frankfurters or Vienna sausages
1 onion, finely chopped
Mustard (Continental)

Paprika
4 small sweet and sour cucumbers
1 small green pepper, chopped
Salt
Fat for frying

Salt the beef. On each slice put a sausage and a cucumber and roll up. Pin each roll with a toothpick. In a large frying pan melt a little fat and add the roulades. When brown all over, place roulades in an oven dish. Fry the onion. When golden brown, add green pepper, and mustard and paprika to taste. Fry for a few more minutes and add to the roulades. Then pour ½ cup of water into frying pan and scrape round the pan to make sauce, bring to the boil and pour over meat. Cover and cook in oven for approximately 1½ hours until the meat is tender. Turn meat regularly. If desired, the onion mixture can be liquidised to make a thicker gravy.

Pickled Spiced Beef

ENGLAND

Serves 8–10　　　**Preparation 5 mins**　　　**Marinate 4 days**　　　**Cook 5 hrs**　　　**Chill 24 hrs**

10 lb brisket of beef (4.5 kg)
8 oz salt (225 g)
2 oz juniper berries (55 g)
2 oz brown sugar (55 g)

2 oz black pepper (55 g)
2 oz saltpetre (55 g)
2 oz allspice (55 g)

Pound all the spices and seasonings together and rub them well into the meat daily for 4 days, turning the meat over each time. Place meat in a saucepan, cover with water, bring to the boil and simmer gently for 5 hours. On removing the meat from the pan place it between two plates, resting a heavy weight on the top plate. Glaze it with the reserved stock the next day when both are quite cold. This meat will keep well for a fortnight.

Rouladen – Swiss Beef Olives

SWITZERLAND   Annette Rose

Serves 8   Preparation 30 mins   Gas No 4, 350°F, 185°C   Cook 2½–3 hrs

8 slices round bola, thinly cut and flattened
8 slices smoked round bola
1 large onion, finely chopped
Pickled cucumbers, in slivers

Large tin tomatoes
Mustard (mild)
Mixed herbs
Salt and pepper

Trim all fat from meat and lay slices flat on kitchen paper. Sprinkle each slice with salt and pepper and spread thinly with mustard. Add a few mixed herbs and 1 teaspoon of chopped onion to each slice, spreading evenly. Divide the smoked bola between the slices so that each one is covered by 1 or 2 pieces of smoked meat. Place a few pickled cucumber slivers towards one end of each slice and roll it up, securing with 1 or 2 wooden cocktail sticks. Place in a large casserole and pour tinned tomatoes over the meat. Cover and cook.

Sauerbraten I

GERMANY   Marianne Durst

Serves 6   **Preparation 20 mins**   **Marinate 2 days**   **Gas No 2½, 310°F, 170°C**
Cook 3½ hrs approx

4 lb piece silverside of beef (1.8 kg)
2 large onions, chopped
6 large tomatoes, chopped
Fat for frying
Flour for thickening
Beef stock cube, if required

Spätzle
Flour
1 egg
Salt and pepper
1 tbls mineral water (approx)

Marinade
1 carrot
1 leek
1 onion, diced
1½ pints red wine (1 litre)
5 tbls vinegar
10 tbls water
2 bay leaves
1 clove
15 peppercorns
½ clove garlic
1 tbls parsley, chopped

Mix all marinade ingredients, cook for 15 minutes then cool. Wash meat thoroughly, checking that all the fat has been removed, and then place in the marinade. Cover completely and leave for at least 2 days in the refrigerator.

Fry chopped onions until brown with tomatoes in some fat in a large pot. Add the beef, reserving the marinade. Brown both sides of the beef and then add enough water to half cover the meat. Then add a little of the marinade, cover and place in the oven for approximately 3 hours. Cook until the meat is soft when tested with a fork, and add water during the cooking as required. When the meat is soft, remove lid and continue to cook until the top of the meat is brown and crisp.

Pour all the juice from the pot through a sieve. Thicken gravy with flour and beef cube if desired or necessary. Place beef back in the pot and pour gravy over it and keep warm until ready to cut into slices (not too thin) and serve with the sauce. Serve with spätzle.

Spätzle: Mix seasoned egg and mineral water with enough flour to make dough. Roll into a sausage shape. Bring a saucepan of water to the boil and with a sharp knife slice the dough into the boiling water then simmer until cooked. Strain and rinse in cold water.

Sauerbraten II

GERMANY   Patricia Mendelson

Serves 8   Preparation 30 mins   Marinate 3 days   Cook 2½–3 hrs

4 lb topside beef (1.8 kg)
¾ pint dry white wine (½ litre)
¼ pint vinegar (120 ml)
1 tsp salt
1 tsp crushed black peppercorns
4 allspice berries
6 tbls margarine
4 tbls flour

2 large onions, sliced
2 large carrots, sliced
2 stalks celery, chopped
½ lemon, sliced
2 bay leaves
4 sprigs parsley
4 cloves
1 tbls brown sugar

Combine wine, vinegar, salt, pepper, onions, lemon, bay leaves, parsley, allspice and cloves. Bring to boil, pour over meat. Cover and refrigerate for 3 days, turning meat daily.

Dry meat and reserve the marinade. Heat 2 tablespoons margarine in a deep pot and seal meat all over. Sprinkle with 2 tablespoons of flour and brown on all sides. Pour in hot marinade, add carrots and celery, cover, lower heat and simmer for 2½–3 hours. Pour off liquid, cool a little, skim off the fat and strain. Melt remaining margarine and blend in remaining flour and sugar and cook slowly until slightly brown. Gradually add strained marinade, stirring until thick and smooth. Pour sauce over meat and serve with red cabbage and 'klose' (see vegetable section).

Semur

INDONESIA   Violet Musry

Serves 6   Marinate 4 hrs   Preparation 15 mins   Cook 1 hr approx

1 cup pineapple juice
3–4 medium onions, sliced
2 lb goulash beef/chicken (900 g)
Dark soya sauce
Sunflower oil for frying
4 large potatoes, cubed

2–3 cloves garlic, crushed
2–3 tomatoes, skinned and quartered
½ tsp nutmeg
¼ tsp cloves
Salt and white pepper

Cut the meat into thin diagonal strips and marinate for 4 hours in pineapple juice. Fry onions in oil until almost brown, add garlic and soya sauce and then the meat, pineapple juice, nutmeg, cloves, pepper, potatoes and tomatoes. Cover and cook, stirring occasionally and making sure that the meat is turned at regular intervals. Add salt to taste after 30 minutes. Check seasonings and serve with plain steamed Basmati rice.

Gevulde Milt – Stuffed Spleen

HOLLAND   Nanny ten Brink-de-Lieme

Serves 6   Preparation 40 mins   Cook 3½ hrs

1 cow's spleen
1 oz margarine or fat (25 g)
5½ oz raw fat (150 g)
1 egg

2 slices white bread
1 onion, finely chopped
1 lb 1 oz flour (500 g)
Salt and pepper

Scrape spleen carefully with a spoon to remove all the bloody texture from the inside of the spleen. Reserve the removed 'studge' so that it can be used in the stuffing. This takes time and you get your hands dirty. Fry the onion in the margarine. Soak the bread slices in water and then squeeze out. Mix onion and bread with the spleen 'studge' and all other remaining ingredients until a coherent substance is reached. Place a small piece in a pan of boiling water – if the piece stays together then the stuffing is good. Fill the spleen with the mixture (not too fast or too full). Sew up the spleen with thick cotton and cook in boiling water or stock for about 3 hours. Cut into thick slices. Serve with boiled potatoes, a green salad and stewed pears.

Suppenfleisch mit Gruner Sosse

GERMANY   Patricia Mendelson

Serves 6   Preparation 15 mins   Cook 2½ hrs   Advance

3½ lb fresh brisket or silverside (1½ kg)
3 carrots
2 onions
1 leek
1 stick celery

Cold sauce
Thin mayonnaise
1 hard boiled egg, finely chopped
Handful of parsley, chopped
Handful of chives, chopped
1 dsp tarragon
1 dsp chervil
Salt and pepper
Lemon juice or water

Boil beef and vegetables in the usual way, adding extra vegetables towards the end of cooking time to be served with the meat if desired. Serve with boiled potatoes and a cold sauce.
Cold sauce: Make a light mayonnaise and thin it down with lemon juice or a little cold water, as desired. Add a large finely chopped hard boiled egg, lots of parsley, chives, a little tarragon and chervil, all very finely chopped to make a 'green' sauce. Adjust seasoning, adding salt, pepper and lemon to taste.

This dish was served with cranberry sauce, a beetroot and raw onion salad and sweet-and-sour cucumbers for Shabbat lunch in Frankfurt.

Sweet and Sour Beef

AUSTRIA   Mrs K. Garland

Serves 2–3   Preparation 15 mins   Gas No 4, 350°F, 185°C   Cook 1 hr   Advance Freezable

1 lb lean prime bola, in 1″ (2.5 cm) cubes (450 g)
2 tbls sugar

1 medium onion, chopped coarsely
2 tbls lemon juice
Salt and pepper

Put onion and sugar in saucepan and cook on a low heat until browned. Add meat and lemon juice and salt and pepper to taste. Cover with cold water and simmer until meat is tender. Or, place in ovenproof dish, cover and bake until soft. Add more lemon juice or sugar to taste if necessary.

Tafelspitz – Boiled Beef Austrian Style

AUSTRIA   Suzy Landes

Serves 6   Preparation 10 mins   Cook 2½ hrs

2½ lb brisket (1.1 kg)
3 pints water (1.5 litres)
Salt to taste
8 whole black peppercorns
2 bay leaves

3 carrots, sliced lengthways
2 parsnips, sliced
1 stalk celery
1 tsp sugar
1 large red onion, unpeeled

Put the whole brisket in salted water. Bring to boil, skim and simmer for 1 hour. Add peppercorns, bay leaves and vegetables, sugar and the onion (the red outer skin gives colour to the stock). Continue to simmer for 1½ hours until meat is tender. Remove meat and slice. Place on heated platter with cooked vegetables. Serve with grated horseradish or chrane.

Lamb

Jewish Lamb with Lemon

TURKEY
Jane Finestone

Serves 6   **Preparation 20 mins**   **Cook 2 hrs approx**

2½ lb lean lamb (1.3 kg)
4 tbls olive oil
1 lemon
10 fl oz hot water (280 ml)
Salt and pepper

¾ tsp cinnamon
3 tsp turmeric
¼ tsp mixed spice
1 tbls honey

Cut lamb into small pieces. Heat oil in a deep pan and brown meat on all sides. Slice lemon thinly and place over meat, add hot water, seasonings and spices. Cover tightly and simmer for 1 hour. Add honey and simmer for a further 30 minutes. Serve with noodles.

Passover Lamb Pie

GREECE

Serves 4–6   Preparation 35 mins   Gas No 4, 350°F, 180°C   Cook 45 mins   Advance

Heart, liver, lungs, intestines of lamb
1 cup olive oil
1 cup water
1½ cups matzo meal
2 eggs, beaten

2 hard boiled eggs, chopped
Salt and pepper
½ cup finely chopped dill and spring
  onions

Clean all the meat thoroughly, washing the intestines inside and out. Chop everything very finely and sauté in a little olive oil, add salt and pepper and reserve.
Pastry: In a large saucepan heat the oil and water to boiling. Remove from heat and add the matzo meal, beaten eggs, salt and pepper. Mix well with a wooden spoon to form a soft dough. Turn out onto a board sprinkled with matzo meal and knead for 2 or 3 minutes. Divide the dough in half and roll out each to a thickness of ¼" (⅔ cm). Line the bottom of a well-greased pie dish with one half of the dough, and pour in the meat mixture. Sprinkle the chopped eggs, dill and spring onions over the meat then cover with the second piece of dough. Seal the edges and make two vents in the top. Bake until well-browned. Can be served hot or cold.

Thoumiyi

IRAQ   'The Scribe'

Serves 4–6   **Preparation 15 mins**   **Cook 1½ hrs**

2 lb lamb, cubed (900 g)
1 bunch spring onions, finely chopped
7 cloves garlic (optional)
5 tbls sugar or to taste
Salt and pepper

1 onion, finely chopped
1 bunch chopped fresh mint
¾ cup lemon juice
1 tbls oil

Salt and pepper the meat. Put in a pan with the oil, onions and garlic. Cook over a medium heat, stirring, until evenly browned. Cover with boiling water and simmer for 1 hour. Add lemon juice and sugar, then the mint. Simmer until all the ingredients are cooked and the taste is sweet and sour and a small amount of thick sauce remains. Serve hot with white rice.

If preferred, garlic cloves can be added halfway through the cooking time; also beef can be used instead of lamb.

Veal

Fried Brains Croquettes

BULGARIA

Serves 4–6　　　**Preparation 20 mins**　　　**Soaking time 30 mins**　　　**Cook 25 mins**

3 calves' brains
1 tbls vinegar
1 onion, chopped
¼ cup stock
½ tsp pepper
3 eggs, beaten
½ cup breadcrumbs

2 cups water
4 oz schmaltz (115 g)
1 slice white bread, trimmed
1 tsp salt
2 tbls chopped parsley
¼ cup flour

Wash the brains. Place in a saucepan with the water and vinegar. Bring to boil and cook for 10 minutes. Drain. Plunge into cold water and set aside for 30 minutes. Drain. Remove the membrane and chop the brains finely. Melt 2 tablespoons of schmaltz in a saucepan. Add the onion and sauté for 10 minutes, stirring frequently. Soak the slice of bread in stock for 5 minutes then squeeze all the liquid out. Combine the brains, sautéed onion, bread, salt, pepper and parsley together, and chop until smooth. Add 2 of the eggs, mixing until well blended. Shape into small croquettes. Dip in flour, then in the remaining egg, and finally in the breadcrumbs. Melt the remaining fat in a saucepan and fry until brown on both sides. Serve at once.

Hot Calf's Foot Sweet and Sour

RUSSIA　　　　　　　　　　　　　　　　　　　　　　　　Guggy Grahame

Serves 3–4　　　　　　　**Preparation 20 mins**　　　　　　　**Cook 2¼ hrs**

1 calf's foot, skinned and broken into pieces
2 pints cold water (1.15 litres)
Salt and pepper
1 dsp sugar
Juice of 1 lemon

1 large carrot
1 small onion
1 stick celery
3 egg yolks
Hot garlic bread slices

Put the calf's foot pieces into a saucepan and cover with cold water. Add salt and pepper and the vegetables. Bring to the boil, skim and leave to simmer on a very low heat, occasionally skimming, until the flesh is soft and comes away from the bone. This takes about 2 hours but can be done more quickly in a pressure cooker if preferred. Remove marrow from the bones and cut or chop the flesh. Put aside and keep hot. Bring the liquid to the boil again. Whisk egg yolks with lemon juice and sugar until smooth. Strain the remaining boiling stock over the egg mixture, constantly whisking, until well mixed. Put the meat on the heated garlic bread slices and pour the liquid over. Eat immediately. May be used as a starter or main course.

Fegato Alla Giudaica

ITALY Elena Grosskopf

Serves 4 **Preparation 5 mins** **Cook 5 mins** **Marinate 3 hrs**

1¾ lb liver, thinly sliced (790 g) Pinch of salt
2 onions, sliced Vegetable oil for frying
1 wineglass of vermouth

Sauté the onions in oil. Add the liver and fry for a few minutes on both sides. Then pour over the glass of vermouth and let it come to the boil. Turn off the heat and leave to marinate. Before serving, sprinkle with salt.

Roast Stuffed Veal

LITHUANIA Rusty Sotnick

Serves 8–10 **Preparation 20 mins** **Gas No 5, 375°F, 190°C** **Cook 1½–2 hrs**

6 lb breast of veal – thick piece (2.7 kg) 2 eggs
Medium matzo meal or fine white 3 carrots, sliced
   breadcrumbs Pinch of nutmeg
2 onions, sliced Salt and pepper
1 tbls ground almonds (optional)
Melted chicken fat

Cut a pocket in the veal, wash it and pat dry. Beat eggs lightly and add 2 tablespoons of chicken fat, seasonings and ground almonds and enough matzo meal or breadcrumbs to make a firm stuffing. Put mixture into pocket in veal. Lay meat in baking tin. Brush with melted fat or a vegetable oil. Pour a little hot water into tin and add sliced onions and carrots. Bake at Gas No 5, 375°F, 190°C for 30 minutes then lower the temperature to Gas No 4, 350°F, 185°C for 1½ hours approximately. Carve downwards. Serve with carrots, parsnips and roast potatoes.

Braised Sweetbreads

SOUTH AFRICA

Serves 3   Soaking time 1¼ hrs   Preparation 15 mins   Gas No 4, 350°F, 185°C
Cook 1¼ hrs

6 sweetbreads (3 pairs)
1 carrot, sliced
1 tbls chopped parsley
1½ cups chicken or beef stock
1 tbls flour

3 tbls schmaltz
1 onion, sliced
1 bay leaf
½ cup white wine
Salt and pepper to taste

Before preparing sweetbreads soak them in cold water for 1 hour and then plunge them into water mixed with lemon juice for 2–3 minutes, and again into the cold water for a few minutes. This will keep them white and firm.

Soak, trim, parboil and season sweetbreads. Melt schmaltz and fry carrot, onion and parsley together with bay leaf. Cook over a medium heat until they start to brown. Then sprinkle the flour over them. Add sweetbreads, wine and stock to vegetables, bring to the boil and then braise in the oven, basting frequently, for 1 hour or until cooked. When they are cooked, sweetbreads start to break when tested with a fork.

Veal Tongue with Olives

ITALY

Serves 6–8   Preparation 15 mins   Cook 3½ hrs

1 pickled veal tongue
11 oz pitted black olives (300 g)
1 tbls tomato paste
1 tbls basil

4 tbls olive oil
1 tsp oregano
1 clove garlic
Freshly ground pepper

Place the tongue in a deep saucepan, cover with cold water and bring to boil. Skim, cover and cook until tender – 3 hours approximately. Take the tongue out of the water, remove skin and all fat. Reserve liquid. Allow the tongue to cool for 15 minutes then cut into very thin slices.

In a small saucepan fry the garlic in the olive oil. When garlic begins to colour, remove and discard it. To the oil add a cup of the reserved cooking liquid, the tomato paste, herbs and seasonings. Slice the olives very thinly, stir them in then add the sliced tongue. The sauce should cover the tongue, but if necessary add a little more of the reserved cooking liquid. Cover the saucepan and simmer for a further 30 minutes. Serve hot.

Minced Meat

Bobotie

SOUTH AFRICA

Serves 3–4   Preparation 15 mins   Gas No 6, 400°F, 200°C   Cook 45 mins

1 lb minced meat (450 g)
1 tbls curry powder
½ cup stock
2 eggs, beaten
Juice of 1 lemon
Oil for frying

2 slices white bread
1 onion, chopped
1 dsp sugar
1 bay leaf
Salt and pepper

Soak bread in stock and squeeze dry. Reserve stock. Fry onion in oil and drain. Mix curry powder, bay leaf, lemon juice, sugar, salt, pepper and fried onions. Mash soaked bread with a fork and then add meat and onion mixture. Beat 1 egg and add to the mixture with half the stock. Press mixture into a pie dish and pour over the other beaten egg to glaze. Stand pie dish in a pan containing ½" (1.25 cm) water and then bake.

Stuffed Cabbage

HUNGARY/ROMANIA   Liz Harris

Serves 6–8   Preparation 30 mins   Cook 3½ hrs   Advance

3 cooking apples, sliced
2 lb minced meat (900 g)
6 oz rice (170 g)
1 tbls sugar
2 tbls vinegar

1 large/2 small tins sauerkraut
2 large onions, chopped
14 oz tin tomatoes (400 g)
1 large white cabbage
Oil for frying

Boil the cabbage gently until you can peel off the leaves. Mix the minced meat with the rice and place a small amount in the centre of each leaf. Roll the leaf over and tuck in both sides to make a neat parcel.
Fry the onions in oil in a large heavy pan until soft. Then add, in layers, sauerkraut, apples and cabbage parcels. Pour over the tinned tomatoes, add sugar and vinegar to the mixture, cover the pan and simmer very gently on top of the cooker for 3 hours. Much better if made one day in advance.

Traditionally cooked for Succot.

Stuffed Cabbage with Apricot Preserves

GERMANY   Minnie Nedas

Serves 6–8   **Preparation 30 mins**   **Cook 1½ hrs**

12 large cabbage leaves
Boiling water to cover
1 lb ground beef (450 g)
2 oz uncooked rice
1 egg
1 grated onion

Salt and pepper to taste
14 oz tin tomatoes (400 g)
Juice of 2 lemons
¾ cup brown sugar
½ cup apricot preserves

Soak leaves in boiling water to soften. Combine meat, rice, egg, onion and seasonings. Drain leaves, place an equal amount of meat mixture on each leaf. Roll up and fasten with toothpick. Place in a deep pan and cover with remaining ingredients. Add enough water to cover, bring to boil and simmer for 1½ hours.

Dolma or Sarma – Stuffed Cabbage

TURKEY   Dolma – Loni Eibenschutz
                                              Sauce – Sylvia Arnstein Mayer

Serves 4   **Preparation 20 mins**   **Cook 1½ hrs**

1 large cabbage
1½ lb minced beef (700 g)
1 teacup rice
1 tbls minced parsley
1 tsp nutmeg
1 clove garlic, crushed
1 medium onion, finely sliced
3 tbls olive oil or seed oil

1 egg, beaten
Salt and pepper
Sauce
1 oz margarine (25 g)
1 tbls flour
1 tbls lemon juice
2 egg yolks

Separate cabbage leaves carefully without breaking them. Bring water to boil in large pot and simmer 4–6 leaves at a time for 2–3 minutes until soft, then drain them in a colander. Thoroughly mix minced meat with the rice, egg, parsley, nutmeg, and salt and pepper. Lay cabbage leaves on table and on the centre of each leaf place about 1 tablespoon of the meat mixture. Wrap the leaves around to form small bundles. Fry the onion and garlic in the oil in a large pot until slightly brown. Take off heat and place cabbage bundles into the pot in layers. Cover with water and bring to boil. Simmer for 1 hour. Remove dolmas and keep warm. Reserve the liquid.
Sauce: Strain the reserved liquid. Melt margarine slowly in a small pot. Stir in the flour, add the liquid, with more hot water if necessary, to obtain a light béchamel. Adjust salt if necessary. Complete sauce by stirring in the egg yolks and lemon juice. Do not boil. Vine leaves can be used instead of cabbage leaves in this recipe.

This is traditionally eaten at Succot.

Empanada Criolla

ARGENTINA   Nicole Davoud

Serves 4   **Preparation 20 mins**   **Cook 20 mins approx**

Pastry   *Filling*
1 lb flour (450 g)   **1 lb minced meat (450 g)**
8 oz white fat or corn oil (225 g)   **2 oz green olives, stoned (50 g)**
1 tsp salt   **1 oz white sultanas (25 g)**
Water to bind   **2 hard boiled eggs, chopped**
***or* 1 lb frozen puff pastry (450 g)**   **1 medium onion, chopped**
                                             Salt and white pepper
                                             Oil for frying

Pastry: Mix flour and fat into breadcrumbs, then add salt water mixture a little at a time to the pastry. When mixed, roll the pastry out fairly thinly. The pastry should be quite dry. Cut pastry into circles the size of a tea-saucer.
Filling: Fry meat in oil with onion, salt and pepper. Once it is light brown remove from heat and add the rest of the ingredients (olives need to be cut into sultana-size pieces). Place mixture on pastry circles and fold over and stick edges together with water. Deep fry on both sides quickly, ensuring the mixture is heated through. The pastry should not be too brown.

Keftele au Bouillon

ROMANIA   Hermy Jankel

Serves 8   **Preparation 15 mins**   **Gas No 4, 350°F, 185°C**   **Cook 1½ hrs**

2–3 lb meat (usually ½ veal, ½ beef), finely   **Salt and pepper**
   minced (1–1.35 kg)   **1 pint water (570 ml)**
4 slices of bread, soaked in water and well   **2 tbls sugar**
   squeezed   **3 eggs**
1–2 tbls flour   **Oil for browning**
5 oz tomato purée (140 g)

Bind meat together with 3 eggs and bread, add salt and pepper. Make into balls and dip in flour. Sauté in oil until evenly brown. Arrange in oven dish. Add flour to remaining oil in the frying pan. Stir, add water, tomato purée and sugar. Mix well and pour over meat balls. Cover with foil and bake.

Koenigsberger Klops

GERMANY   Mrs I Ryz

Serves 6   **Preparation 10 mins**   **Cook 1½ hrs**

1½ lb minced meat (675 g)
Medium matzo meal
1 soupspoon parsley, chopped
3 pints meat stock (2 litres)
2 eggs, lightly beaten

1 soupspoon tomato ketchup
1 onion, grated
Salt and pepper
Gravy
2 tbls flour or cornflour
Capers (optional)

Mix all ingredients together except the stock and cornflour, adding enough matzo meal to make a smooth sticky dough. With wet hands form the mixture into balls. The mixture should not crumble. Bring the stock to the boil and drop the balls into it. Simmer for 15 minutes then remove the balls and reserve.

To make the gravy, mix cornflour with a little water until smooth, then bring to the boil. Add the meat balls and some of the stock, cover and simmer for 1 hour. Capers can be added to the gravy.

Matzo Bake

EGYPT   Doris Afif

Serves 4–6   **Preparation 20 mins**   **Gas No 6, 400°F, 200°C**   **Cook 30 mins approx**

1 box of matzos
2 lb minced beef (900 g)
6 large eggs, beaten
1 clove garlic, crushed
1 chicken stock cube

½ pint hot water (285 ml)
1 tsp salt
1 small onion, chopped
Salt and pepper to taste

Half fill a large bowl (big enough to place a matzo in without breaking it) with cold water and then add a teaspoon of salt. Dip each matzo in the water for a couple of minutes and then drain thoroughly. Place on a teacloth for 10 minutes until each matzo is soft and pliable. Leave matzos to one side. Fry the minced beef with the crushed garlic, salt, pepper and onion until cooked and dried. Also put to one side. Place a layer of matzos at the bottom of an ovenproof dish and brush each piece with beaten egg. Continue doing this until you have used about ⅓ of the matzos. Then add the cooked beef and then finish off with the rest of the matzos, always brushing each slice with beaten egg. Brush the top layer of matzos with extra egg to give a shiny finish and then cut into squares. Cook in a pre-heated oven, occasionally basting with stock made by dissolving the cube in the ½ pint water. When golden brown, remove the dish from the oven and serve with pickles and salad.

This is a popular Passover recipe.

Meat Balls in Vine Leaves

ROMANIA　　　　　　　　　　　　　　　　　　　　　Jewels Leader Cramer

Serves 10–12　　**Preparation 25 mins**　　**Gas No 3, 325°F, 180°C**　　**Cook 1½–2 hrs**

36 large fresh vine leaves *or* 1 packet vine
　leaves in brine
1 dsp sugar or more to taste
1 cup long grain rice
1¾ pints tomato juice (1 litre)

12 large tomatoes
Juice of 1 lemon
Salt and pepper
1½ lb minced meat (675 g)

If vine leaves are fresh, soak in boiling water until soft. If using a packet of vine leaves soak in boiling water for 10 minutes. Rinse vine leaves after soaking and reserve. Mix meat with rice, salt and pepper and reserve. Cut tops off tomatoes and scoop out flesh. Liquidise flesh with sugar, tomato juice and lemon juice. Fill the tomato skins with the meat and rice mixture and then replace tops of tomatoes. Make parcels of the vine leaves with the meat and rice mixture inside. Place the stuffed tomatoes and vine leaves in a casserole, pour over the liquidised juice and cook.

This dish was used by the Yager family in Romania. I inherited the recipe and have continued to cook it over the years for family and friends.

Medias – Stuffed Vegetables

SUDAN　　　　　　　　　　　　　　　　　　　　　　　　Ruth Synett

Serves 6　　**Preparation 30 mins**　　**Gas No 4, 350°F, 185°C**　　**Cook 1 hr**

3 medium aubergines
3 beef tomatoes
3 tbls breadcrumbs or matzo meal
1 tsp mixed spice
1 egg
4 tbls tomato purée
3 medium courgettes

1 lb minced beef or lamb (450 g)
1 tsp cinnamon

For frying
1 egg
Matzo meal
Oil

Combine meat with egg, breadcrumbs and spices and mix well. Cut the aubergines and courgettes in half lengthways and cut the tomatoes simply in half. Scoop out the centres and reserve. Fill the vegetables with the meat mixture, pressing it in well.
For frying: Beat the egg. Dip the stuffed vegetables in the egg and then in the matzo meal and fry in oil on both sides until lightly browned and sealed.
Place the reserved vegetable centres in a baking dish and put the stuffed vegetables on top. Dilute the tomato purée with water and pour over the vegetables to cover. Place a plate on top to keep vegetables down and cover with lid. Bake for approximately 1 hour until most of the liquid is absorbed. Serve with rice.

Meat Filo

EGYPT   Mrs Cadranel

Serves 3   Preparation 30 mins   Gas No 3, 325°F, 180°C   Cook 15–20 mins

1 lb 2 oz filo pastry (500 g)
Oil
Sesame seeds

Filling
1 lb 2 oz minced steak (500 g)
3 tbls oil
1 onion, minced
½ cup water
1 egg, beaten
Salt and pepper

Heat oil and brown onion and meat. Add water and simmer until meat is cooked. Add seasoning and cool. Mix in beaten egg. Cut one sheet of filo in three strips. Brush one strip of filo with oil and fold in two. Place one dessertspoonful of filling at one end and fold into a triangular shape. Brush with oil and sprinkle with seasame seeds. Repeat with remaining pastry. Bake.

Meat Keema

INDIA   Mavis Hyman

Serves 4   Preparation 15 mins   Gas No 4, 350°F, 185°C   Cook 45 mins   Advance

1 lb minced beef, lamb or chicken (450 g)
3 tbls vegetable oil
1 cup celery, chopped
2 tsp fresh ginger, grated
½ tsp garlic, grated
3 large onions, chopped

1 cup white cabbage, shredded
1 cup carrots, chopped
½ tsp turmeric powder
A few green chillies, chopped (optional)
Garnish
Coriander leaves, chopped

Fry meat in the oil until cooked through. Add all other ingredients and mix thoroughly. Cook in an uncovered ovenproof dish for 45 minutes. Remove from oven and garnish with coriander. Serve with chutney.

Kibbeh

SYRIA

Serves 4–6   **Preparation 25 mins**   **Cook 20 mins**

8 oz medium matzo meal (225 g)
2 tbls ground rice
½ onion, minced
½ tsp ground cumin
Salt and pepper to taste
Warm water
Oil for frying

Filling
1 lb chicken, lamb or beef, finely minced
  (450 g)
1 large onion, finely minced
Salt and black pepper
4 oz cracked wheat (115 g)
1–2 tbls cold water
¼ tsp ground coriander
Pinch turmeric

Mix matzo meal, ground rice, onion, cumin, salt and pepper together, using enough warm water to make a stiff paste. Mix all the meat filling ingredients together. Form matzo paste into large balls and make a hole in the middle of each. Fill with the meat filling and reseal. Deep fry until crisp and golden.

This recipe was traditionally served at Passover.

Stuffed Peppers I

HUNGARY   Tania Slowe

Serves 4   Preparation 15 mins   Gas No 4, 350°F, 185°C   Cook 30 mins approx

1 lb minced meat, all beef
  or ½ beef, ½ veal (450 g)
4 green peppers
½ large onion, finely chopped
1 cup cooked white rice
1 egg, beaten
Mustard

2 tbls parsley, finely chopped
Salt and pepper to taste
Sauce
1 large onion, finely chopped
Vegetable oil for frying
Salt and pepper
2 medium or 1 large tin tomatoes

Remove the cores and seeds from the peppers, taking care not to split them. Wash them well inside and out, and stand them upside down to drain. Add rice to minced meat, egg, onion, mustard (1 heaped teaspoon if using French mustard or less if using English), parsley and salt and pepper to taste. Mix thoroughly. Fill the peppers with the meat and rice mixture but to not pack the stuffing too tightly or the peppers may burst during cooking. Shape any leftover mixture into meat balls. These can be cooked alongside the peppers.

Make a tomato sauce by frying the onion in a little vegetable oil until soft. Add the tomatoes, breaking them up with a wooden spoon. Season with salt and pepper. Cook over a medium heat for ten minutes.

Place the stuffed peppers and meat balls in the sauce, cover and cook in a gentle oven until the peppers are tender, by which time the stuffing will also be cooked. If the sauce is too liquid, remove the cooked peppers and meat balls and reduce the sauce over a high heat until thickened. Serve with plain boiled potatoes.

Stuffed Green Peppers II

MEXICO

Serves 6   **Preparation 15 mins**   **Cook 30 mins approx**

6 large green peppers   12 oz lean minced beef (340 g)
¼ cup oil   3 tbls tomato paste
1 clove garlic, minced   2 tsp chilli powder
1 tsp salt   3 tbls ground almonds or peanuts
¼ cup flour   2 eggs, beaten
1 cup fine breadcrumbs   Oil or shmaltz for deep frying

Cut tops off peppers, remove seeds and membranes, and place in a saucepan with sufficient water to cover. Bring to the boil, and immediately drain. Cool for a few minutes.

Heat the oil in a pan, and add the beef, tomato paste, garlic, chilli powder, salt and ground nuts. Sauté over a low heat, stirring constantly for 5 minutes. Correct seasoning and set aside.

Stuff the peppers with the meat mixture, and sprinkle flour on the peppers at the open end. Dip each pepper in beaten egg, then in breadcrumbs, and again in the egg and then in the breadcrumbs. Heat fat or oil in a deep saucepan. Place one or two peppers at a time in the hot fat. Fry until browned and drain. Serve hot.

Syngatu

YUGOSLAVIA   Henaki Konforte

Serves 2–3   **Preparation 20 mins**   **Cook 10 mins**

1 lb 2 oz leeks (500 g)   1 tbls oil
10 oz minced beef (300 g)   Flour
1 egg   Oil for frying
Salt and white pepper

Cut leeks in thin slices and boil for 15 minutes, then drain and mince. Add the meat, 1 tablespoon of oil, salt and pepper and egg. Mix thoroughly together and then make into burger shapes about 2½″ (6 cm) in diameter. Dip them into flour and deep fry on a medium heat. Serve hot with boiled potatoes or cold if preferred.

Potato Chips with Chicken or Meat Filling

INDIA   Sally Silas/Tabby Corre

Serves 12–15   **Preparation 20 mins**   **Cook 40 mins**

12 large potatoes
4 onions, finely chopped
1 tsp ginger
1 tsp parsley or coriander, chopped
1 large tomato, chopped
Beaten egg for coating
Oil for frying

1 lb chicken or meat, minced (450 g)
1 tsp garlic, finely chopped
1 tsp garam masala
1 tsp turmeric
¼ cup oil
Breadcrumbs for coating

Boil potatoes, strain and mash. Add salt to the potatoes and set aside. Fry onions in oil until brown and then add tomato and stir well. Add minced chicken (or meat) and spices and fry together. Half cover the frying pan and cook on a medium heat until the liquid is absorbed, stir in parsley (or coriander) and allow to cool. Take mashed potato and divide into balls making a hollow in each ball. Put 1 dessertspoon of cooled filling mixture in hollow and then close ball. Shape into oval or round patties. When finished, roll patties first in beaten egg and then in breadcrumbs. Fry in oil and serve.

Shefta

INDIA   Violet Musry

Serves 6   **Preparation 15 mins**   **Refrigerate 2 hrs**   **Gas No 5, 375°F, 190°C**
Cook 20 mins

2 lb minced lamb or beef, with a little fat
    (900 g)
2 handfuls parsley, chopped
3 medium onions, chopped

Sweet paprika
A little olive oil
Salt and pepper to taste
Wooden sticks

Mix all ingredients together and leave in the refrigerator for 2 hours. Mould mixture on to wooden sticks in long sausage shapes approximately 4″ × 1″ (10 × 2.5 cm) thick and place on a greased tray (you can remove sausages from sticks before cooking if desired). Cook in oven or under grill on one side only. Serve with pitta bread or rice and chopped salad with lots of lemon juice.

POULTRY

Baghdadi Jewish Style Pot-Roasted Chicken

INDIA

Serves 8   **Preparation 10 mins**   **Cook 1¾ hrs approx**

2 roasting chickens, jointed
5–6 cloves garlic, peeled
2 large onions, chopped
1½ tsp turmeric
1 cup water

2 tbls oil
2 cinnamon sticks
3 bay leaves
2 tsp salt
1½ tsp black peppercorns

Place all ingredients in a heavy pan, mixing until the turmeric is distributed through-out. Cover and cook for approximately 1 hour until nearly done. Remove cover and cook on moderate heat until water has evaporated and chicken is tender. Chicken will stick to the bottom of the pan as it browns in the accumulated fat and oil. Cool in the pan and serve with the browned side up, either at room temperature or slightly warmer. Serve chicken with Mehti chutney.

Chicken Paprikash

CZECHOSLOVAKIA   Jackie Gryn

Serves 4   **Preparation 10 mins**   **Cook 1 hr**

1 small roasting chicken, cut into 8 pieces
2 tsp paprika
1 green pepper, diced
14 oz tin of peeled tomatoes (440 g)
1 lb onions, sliced (450 g)

Chicken fat or oil for frying
1 dsp tomato purée
Flour to coat
Salt and pepper to taste

Sweat onion in fat until translucent. Remove to a plate. Remove skin from chicken joints and coat with seasoned flour. Brown chicken in fat and then add onions, seasoning, tomatoes, tomato purée, paprika and green pepper. Simmer for 1 hour. Garnish with parsley.

Chicken Sefreeto

EGYPT   Bella Cohen-Setton

Serves 4–6   **Preparation 15 mins**   **Cook 2 hr approx**   **Advance**

3½–4 lb chicken (2 kg)
1 clove garlic, chopped
Salt and pepper
Lemon
Potatoes as required

1 onion, sliced
1 cup oil
1 tsp powdered turmeric
4 cups chicken stock

Place oil in a large casserole and fry garlic and onion until lightly browned. Then brown the chicken (either in pieces or whole), add seasoning, turmeric, a squeeze of lemon and chicken stock. Simmer on very low heat for 45 minutes then turn the chicken over. Add potatoes cut into cubes and simmer for another 30 minutes. Serve with rice.

Chiturney – Sweet-Sour Chicken Curry

INDIA   Edwina Slotover

Serves 6–8   **Preparation 20 mins**   **Gas No 4, 350°F, 185°C**   **Cook 1½ hrs**   **Advance**

5 lb chicken, cut into portions (2¼ kg)
2 tbls oil
3 large onions, finely sliced
2 tsp garlic powder
2 tsp ginger paste
1 tsp turmeric
1 tsp curry paste
2 tbls desiccated coconut

1 tbls tamarind paste
14 oz tin tomatoes (400 g)
5 oz jar tomato purée (140 g)
1¾ pints chicken stock (1 litre)
1 tbls sugar
Salt and pepper
Bunch of coriander leaves

Heat the oil in a large saucepan. Sauté the chicken pieces and place in a deep casserole. Season with garlic powder, cover and set aside. In the saucepan sauté the onions. When translucent and soft add the ginger, turmeric and curry paste and cook for 3–4 minutes, stirring continuously. Add the tinned tomatoes, tomato purée, chicken stock, tamarind, desiccated coconut and sugar and stir well. Cover and cook for 10 minutes to blend the flavours. Taste the gravy and adjust the seasonings and all spices to taste. The curry should have a rich sweet-sour, slightly spicy flavour. If too sharp, add more sugar. When satisfied with the flavour, pour the gravy over the chicken pieces, add the coriander leaves, cover and cook in the oven for 1 hour or until chicken is tender. This recipe is best cooked a day in advance to allow the flavours to be absorbed by the chicken.

Chiturney was traditionally served for Friday night dinner in Bombay.

Egyptian Lemon Chicken

EGYPT   Deanne Simon

Serves 6–8 Marinate 2 hrs Preparation 10 mins Gas No 4, 350°F, 185°C Cook 1 hr

2 small chickens, portioned
4 oz margarine (115 g)
2 tbls parsley

Marinade
4 tbls olive oil
1 clove garlic, crushed
Grated rind and juice of 1 lemon (approx 2 tbls)
¼ tsp dried thyme
Salt and freshly ground pepper

Marinate the chicken portions in marinade ingredients for at least 2 hours. Make tiny nicks in the skin of the chicken to allow marinade to permeate chicken. Place chicken in casserole dish or roasting tin and dot with margarine. Pour over marinade and cook uncovered until tender. Cover with foil if it appears to be drying out. Remove from oven and sprinkle with freshly chopped parsley. Serve with rice, a middle-eastern vegetable such as stuffed onions and a green vegetable.

False Fish

HUNGARY   Aniko Grunsfeld

Serves 3–4   Preparation 20 mins   Gas No 4, 350°F, 185°C   Cook 1 hr   Advance

1 large breast of boiling or roasting chicken, minced
1 small onion, grated
2 cloves garlic, grated
1 slice cholla
1 egg, beaten
Salt and pepper to taste

Sauce
1 carrot, sliced
1 onion, sliced
2 sticks of celery, chopped
Salt and pepper
½ tsp paprika
15 fl oz water (425 ml)

In a bowl, mix together chicken, onion, garlic, egg and seasonings. Soak cholla in water, press to remove excess water and add to chicken mixture. With wet hands, form into balls.
Sauce: Cook carrots, onions and celery in water with salt, pepper and paprika for 30 minutes. Pour sauce over the chicken balls and simmer for a further 20 minutes.
Place chicken balls on a platter, garnish with the vegetables and pour sauce around. Cool and serve.

Hameem

INDIA   Sally Silas/Tabby Corre

Serves 6–8   Preparation 30 mins   Gas No ¼, 225°F, 120°C   Cook overnight

F ameem
1 chicken
2 tomatoes, chopped
2 cups rice, washed
Chicken fat or oil for frying
2 onions, finely sliced

F ashwa (stuffing)
1 cup rice
2 tomatoes, chopped
¼ chicken breast, boned and cubed
Salt and pepper
5 pods cardamom
2 tsp cinnamon

Skin and cut the chicken, leaving the back and wings intact, but separating the legs and thighs and portioning the breasts. Reserve the skin. Mix all the stuffing ingredients together and stuff the chicken skin with the mixture; sew up open ends of the skin. In a large saucepan, heat the oil or fat and sauté the onions and tomatoes. Add the chicken pieces and cook for 5 minutes. Place the hashwa in the centre of the pan and surround with rice. Add boiling water to cover and simmer for 15 minutes. Place in oven and cook overnight.

This dish was traditionally eaten for Shabbat lunch.

Jewelled Rice with Chicken

IRAN/PERSIA   Maryam Zenoubian

Serves 6   Preparation 40 mins   Soaking time (optional) 2 hrs   Cook 1¾ hrs

3 cups long grain rice
3 lb roasting chicken, jointed (1.35 kg)
2 onions, chopped
2 tbls plus ½ tsp salt
1 cup finely slivered orange peel
2 carrots, cut into long slivers
1 cup sugar

1 cup raisins
1 cup washed, dried barberries
½ cup oil
½ tsp ground saffron, dissolved in 2 tbls
   hot water
2 tbls slivered almonds
2 tbls pistachios

Clean and wash rice in cold water until water is clear. (If desired, it may then be soaked with 2 tablespoons salt for 2 hours.) Place chicken and 1 chopped onion in a pan, add ½ teaspoon salt. Cover and simmer for 45 minutes over low heat. Do NOT add water. Bone chicken and cut into pieces. Reserve juices. Cover orange peel with water, bring to boil and drain to remove bitter taste. Place orange peel, carrot strips, sugar and 1 cup of water in pan and boil for 10 minutes. Drain and set aside. Sauté 1 chopped onion, raisins and barberries in a little oil for 2 minutes. Add orange peel and carrot mixture and set aside. In a large non-stick pot, bring to boil 8 cups water with 2 tablespoons salt. Add clean rice and boil briskly for 6 minutes, stirring occasionally. Drain and rinse in lukewarm water. Place 2 tablespoons of rice back in the pot, add a few pieces of chicken: repeat and shape rice into pyramid. Pour over remaining oil, saffron and 2 tablespoons chicken juices. Cover pot with a cloth and cook 10 minutes over medium heat and 50 minutes over low heat. Remove from heat and allow to cool for 5 minutes without removing cover. Set aside 2 tablespoons saffron flavoured rice for garnish. With a large spoon, layer rice alternately with chicken and barberry mixture on an oval platter. Shape into a cone, decorate top with the rice set aside for garnish, some barberry mixture, and the almonds and pistachios.

Roast Chicken with Honey

JAMAICA   Diana Battat

Serves 4–6   Preparation 10 mins   Gas No 4, 350°F, 185°C   Cook 1 hr approx

1 large chicken, cut into portions
½ cup clear honey
½ cup prepared mustard

2 heaped tsp curry powder
Salt to taste

Place chicken pieces in an ovenproof baking dish. Combine the remaining ingredients, mixing well, and pour them over the chicken. Bake in a moderate oven.

Sambusak El Tawa – Chicken Fritters

IRAQ   A Baghdadi Cook

Serves 8–10   Preparation 30 mins   Resting time 30 mins   Cook 1½ hrs   Freezable

Filling
1 roasting chicken
1 small onion
4 large onions, thinly sliced
¼ tsp ground turmeric
½ tsp salt
1 pinch pepper
6 tbls cooking oil
1 tsp ground cumin
1 cup cooked chickpeas

Dough
3 cups unbleached flour
½ cup wholewheat flour
½ tsp salt
2 tbls oil
2 cups oil for deep frying

Dough: Add oil to the flour and salt and mix well (if necessary add 1 or 2 tablespoons of water to make dough more pliable). Let it rest for 30 minutes.

Filling: Place chicken in pot with small onion, turmeric, salt and pepper and cover with boiling water. Bring to boil and skim, simmer until tender (approximately 1 hour). Remove from heat, bone and skin chicken and cut into small bite-size pieces. Reserve. Grind the chickpeas. Fry large, sliced onions, with more turmeric and pepper, in oil until golden. Reduce heat and add cumin and chickpeas and salt to taste. Mix thoroughly. Remove from heat. Add chicken pieces to onion and chickpeas mixture. Cut dough into walnut-size pieces. Roll into balls and roll out each ball into a 3″ circle about ¼″ (7½ × ½ cm) thick. Put 1 tablespoon of chicken mixture in centre of dough, bring edges together and seal tightly with a little water. Place on greased sheet. Heat oil in deep pan until very hot. Reduce heat to medium low. Cook fritters in batches, without overcrowding them, until evenly golden. Serve hot or cold. The fritters can be frozen before frying if desired.

This dish is traditionally served at Purim.

Shola

RUSSIA   Rosa Pine

Serves 6   **Preparation 20 mins**   **Cook 1¼ hrs approx**

4 tbls oil
1 large Spanish onion, chopped
1 roasting chicken, cut into small pieces
2 lb ripe tomatoes, chopped (900 g)
2 cups water
2½ cups risotto or long grain rice

2 carrots, cut into julienne strips
1 bunch fresh coriander
Juice of 2 lemons
Salt to taste
Dash of pepper

Heat oil in a large saucepan and fry onion until golden brown. Add chicken and carrots and continue to cook for a few minutes. Add the water and cook for a further 10 minutes. Add the tomatoes, rice and salt and cook over a gentle heat until the water has evaporated. If the rice is not yet cooked, add another half cup of water and cook until this evaporates. Remove from heat and add lemon juice, pepper and chopped coriander, mix thoroughly and serve.

Stuffed Chicken with Almonds

MOROCCO   Esther Bloomberg

Serves 6   **Preparation 45 mins**   **Gas No 4, 350°F, 185°C**   **Cook 1¾ hrs**

4½ lb chicken with giblets (2.2 kg)
1 cup chicken stock
6 oz unblanched almonds (170 g)
1 cup medium matzo meal/cholla
½ medium onion, chopped
Rind of 1 lemon, finely grated

½ tsp salt
1 heaped tbls sugar
3 × size 2 eggs, beaten
1 carrot, chopped
Saffron (optional)

Prepare the chicken stock using giblets and neck, the carrot and onion. Grill the chicken liver, chop roughly and set aside. Pour boiling water over the almonds and leave to soak for 15 minutes. Peel and grind (prepacked ground almonds DO NOT have the same flavour). In a bowl, mix matzo meal with 1 cup of boiling strained giblet stock. Mixing well with a fork, add ground almonds, the meat from the giblets and neck, chopped, the chicken liver, lemon rind, salt, sugar, eggs and a little saffron (optional). Loosen the skin from the breast of the chicken and insert the stuffing under the skin. With needle and thread secure upper flap of skin to the lower – rub the outside of the chicken with a little oil, adding saffron if desired, and roast.

Tabyeet or Tannouri – Baked Chicken with Rice

IRAQ   Yvonne Aghassidor

Serves 4   Soaking time 2 hrs   Preparation 15 mins   Gas No 6, 400°F, 200°C
Cook 4 hrs

2 cups long grain rice
2 tbls plus 1 tsp salt
1 roasting chicken
4 tbls chicken fat or margarine
2 cardamom pods or ¼ tsp ground
    cardamom

⅛ tsp freshly ground black pepper
Pinch of ground cloves
4 cups boiling water
1 tsp tomato paste
Pinch of cinnamon
⅛ tsp ground turmeric

Wash rice and soak in hot water with 2 tablespoons of salt for 2 hours or overnight.
Wash the chicken thoroughly. Put the fat in a large heavy-bottomed pan. Add pepper
and turmeric and place over high heat until very hot. Reduce the heat to medium. Add
the chicken and sauté lightly on all sides, then add the boiling water, 1 teaspoon salt,
tomato paste and remaining spices. Cook for about 30 minutes. Transfer the chicken
from the pot onto a plate. Reserve liquid.
Drain and add the rice to the reserved liquid. Cook for about 10 minutes or until all the
liquid is absorbed. Put the chicken in the centre of the rice, forcing it to the bottom of
the pot. Place in a moderately hot oven (Gas No 6, 400°F 200°C) for 30 minutes, then
reduce the heat to Gas No2, 250°F 140°C and bake for 2–3 hours. A hard crust will form
at the bottom of the pot. Remove the pot from the oven, sprinkle 2 tablespoons cold
water on top of the rice, cover, and allow to stand for 2–3 minutes (this helps to loosen
the bottom crust).
Lift out the chicken and place it in the centre of a large round platter. Spoon out the rice
and heap around the chicken. Remove the hard crust with a spatula and arrange on top
of the rice.

Variations

Top the Tabyeet with eggs. Wash as many eggs as needed. Before putting the chicken and
rice in the oven, place a piece of aluminium foil on top of the rice. Put the eggs, in their
shells, on the foil and fold the foil over them. The egg whites will be golden brown and
ready to serve when the rice is cooked. These baked eggs are very good for sandwiches
and cocktail canapés, and go especially well with pickles, fresh herbs and salads.
Stuffing the chicken before putting it in the pot. Combine ¼ cup of soaked rice, the finely
chopped giblets, a pinch each of ground cardamom, cinnamon, cloves, pepper,
turmeric and salt, and a few rose petals. Mix well and use to stuff the chicken; sew up
the opening. While the chicken is cooking prick it occasionally with a fork so that some
of the cooking liquid will be absorbed by the stuffing. If the chicken is stuffed *do not add*
cardamom, cinnamon or cloves to the cooking liquid.

*This dish was usually prepared in advance for the Shabbat. It was cooked on Friday afternoon and
placed on very low embers to keep it warm until the next day. Eggs were frequently baked on top of
the rice for breakfast.*

Tebid

IRAQ   Rosa Eshkeri

Serves 6–8   Soaking time 1 hr   Preparation 30 mins   Gas No 6, 400°F, 200°C
Cook 12 hrs

5½–6 lb boiling chicken (2½ kg)   *Stuffing*
10 oz tomato purée (290 g)   ½ glass basmati rice
4 glasses rice   1 medium onion, chopped
2–3 tsp salt   Giblet and heart of chicken, chopped
1 tbls chicken fat   1 medium tomato, chopped
Pepper to taste   2–3 cardamom pods, chopped
                                          Salt, pepper and ground cinnamon to taste
                                          1–2 tsp tomato purée

Soak rice in water for 1 hour.
Stuffing: Soak basmati rice in water for one hour, drain and then mix with all other
stuffing ingredients. Fill the chicken with the stuffing and sew up the opening. Place in
an ovenproof casserole or saucepan which has been rinsed but not dried. Fry in the
chicken fat, making sure all sides are equally browned, then add tomato purée and
cook for a further 5–10 minutes. Add drained rice and sufficient boiling water just to
cover rice. Boil until all water has evaporated. Place casserole in a hot oven (Gas No 6,
400°F, 200°C) and cook for about 30 minutes, then turn the heat down to Gas No ½,
250°F, 140°C and cook overnight.

This dish was a traditional Iraqi Shabbat lunch.

Wiener Backhendl – Chicken A La Wiener Schnitzel

AUSTRIA   Suzy Landes

Serves 6–8   Preparation 10 mins   Gas No 6, 400°F, 200°C   Cook 1 hr

4½ lb chicken, cut into 8 pieces (2 kg)   2 eggs, lightly beaten
½ cup flour   ½ cup breadcrumbs
Salt and pepper to taste

Dip chicken pieces in the flour, then in the lightly beaten eggs and finally in the
breadcrumbs to which salt and pepper have been added. Preheat oven. Pour a little oil
in a dish and place in oven. When oil is hot, add chicken pieces and cook in oven for
about 1 hour, until chicken is crisp. Turn chicken pieces over after 30 minutes.

Stuffed Neck

POLAND   Greta Goldwater

Serves 4–6   **Preparation 10 mins**   **Gas No 5, 375°F, 190°C**   **Cook 1 hr**

Neck of a chicken   **Unrendered chicken fat**
1 onion, chopped (plus ½ tsp finely grated)   **Flour to bind**
Salt and white pepper   **Chicken stock (optional)**

Cook the finely grated onion in chicken fat until soft but not brown. Season with salt and pepper and add enough flour to bind. Mix well, stuff inside chicken neck and sew up. Cook in hot oven in a baking dish with a little water and the rest of the onion, or simmer in chicken soup.

Roast Goose

GERMANY   Ilse Edwards

Serves 6–8   **Preparation 20 mins**   **Gas No 7, 425°F, 220°C**   **Cook 4½ hrs**

1 goose   **Boiling water**
Salt   **Pepper**

After cleaning and washing well, salt and pepper the goose on the inside only. Prick the outside all over with a fork. Put the goose in an oven dish, breast down and pour over approximately 2 pints of boiling water (1 litre). It should be 1½″ (4 cm) deep in the pan. Put in a hot oven for 1 hour. Discard all the water and add the same quantity of fresh boiling water. Return to the oven for a further 30 minutes. Turn over and cook for another 2 hours and 40 minutes. Remove and discard half the liquid. Pour a glass of cold water over the bird. Return to the oven for a further 20 minutes until crisp.

El-Hamam Dil'Arusa – Stuffed Pigeon

ISRAEL/PALESTINE

Serves 4   **Preparation 30 mins**   **Gas No 6, 400°F, 200°C**   **Cook 1¼ hrs**

2 large pigeons
2 fl oz oil (55 ml)

Stuffing
8 oz rice or burgul (225 g)
4 oz lean minced meat, either lamb or veal
    or a combination (115 g)
2 small onions, chopped
2 oz large seedless raisins, chopped (55 g)
5 prunes, soaked and chopped
6 dried apricots, soaked and chopped
1 egg
2 oz chopped roasted nuts (55 g)
4 tbls olive oil
6 tbls chopped parsley

1½ tsp mace
½ tsp cinnamon
¼ tsp ginger
¼ tsp nutmeg
Salt and black pepper

Sauce
2 small onions, chopped
4 oz raisins (115 g)
1 tbls good honey
8 fl oz water (225 ml)
Juice of small lemon
Salt and pepper
A few strands of saffron

Stuffing: Sauté the onions in olive oil. If using rice, place in boiling salted water for 5 minutes and then drain. If using burgul, soak in hot water for 30 minutes and then drain. Mix all stuffing ingredients well and fill cavities of pigeons with it. Any remaining stuffing can be steamed in a mould separately.

Brown the pigeons in 2 fluid ounces of oil (55 ml), remove and keep warm.

Sauce: Add the onion to the oil left in the pan and sweat gently until it starts to colour. Add the honey, raisins, saffron, salt, pepper and water, bring to the boil and simmer for a few minutes.

Place the pigeons in a roasting dish. Pour over sauce, cover and place in oven for 35 minutes, basting frequently. Remove the pigeons and keep hot. Drain some of the fat from the sauce, add the lemon juice and then boil the sauce until it is glossy and slightly thickened. Pour the sauce over the pigeons and serve.

Pigeons have been eaten in Israel since Biblical times. They were served on special occasions, particularly weddings.

Turkey Mole

MEXICO Sheila Swindon

Serves 8 **Preparation 20 mins** **Gas No 8, 450°F, 230°C** **Cook 2 hrs**

8 lb turkey, cut into 8 portions
12 oz onion, finely chopped (340 g)
3 tomatoes, skinned, seeded and chopped
3 oz chopped sultanas (85 g)
½ tsp ground coriander
1 tsp cayenne pepper
2 garlic cloves, finely chopped
½ tsp ground cloves
¼ tsp black pepper

½ tsp salt
3 oz finely chopped almonds (85 g)
15 fl oz boiling chicken stock (425 ml)
4 tbls chicken fat
½ tsp ground cinnamon
1½ oz plain, unsweetened chocolate (45 g)
Garnish
Sesame seeds

Place the turkey pieces in a large saucepan, cover with water and lid and cook on a high heat for 15 minutes. Reduce to medium heat and cook for a further 45 minutes. Meanwhile, combine onion, tomatoes, sultanas, coriander, cayenne, garlic, cinnamon, cloves, almonds, salt, pepper, and stock in a large wooden bowl and mix to a purée.

In a large frying pan, melt the fat gently, add the onion mixture and cook for 5 minutes stirring constantly. Stir in the chocolate until it has dissolved. Drain the turkey pieces and pat dry. Place them in a large ovenproof dish and bake on a high heat, uncovered, for 30 minutes. Cover the turkey with the sauce, lower the heat to Gas No 4, 350°F, 185°C and cook for a further 30 minutes. Before serving sprinkle with sesame seeds.

SNACKS

Cheese Borekas

EGYPT   Bella Cohen-Setton

Serves 4–6   **Preparation 15 mins**   **Cook 5 mins**

8 oz cooking or cottage cheese (225 g)   Squeeze of lemon juice
1 egg for mixture   4 matzos
1 medium-size potato, boiled   1 beaten egg for coating
½ tsp mixed spice   Oil for frying
Salt and pepper

Mix all ingredients, except matzos, to form a paste. Soak the matzos in water and then drain. Sandwich half the filling between two matzos, dip in beaten egg. Repeat with remaining matzos. Deep fry until browned.

Traditionally served at Passover.

Cheese Dumplings

AUSTRIA   Dorothy Pressburg

Serves 2   **Preparation 10 mins**   **Standing time 1 hr**   **Cook 10 mins**

8 oz curd cheese (225 g)   Pinch of salt
2 heaped tbls semolina
2 heaped tbls plain flour   *Topping*
1 size 2 egg   Sugar and ground cinnamon to taste
3 oz sugar (85 g)   2 oz melted butter (55 g)

Mix all ingredients together. Let mixture stand for 1 hour. In a large saucepan bring water to boil and add a pinch of salt. Make small dumplings (about 1" diameter (2.5 cm)), then drop into boiling water. Make sure they do not stick to the saucepan. Once they have risen to the top, let them simmer for 5–8 minutes approximately. When cooked, remove with perforated spoon. Sprinkle with sugar and cinnamon and pour over the melted butter. Serve at once.

Cheese Kreplach

RUSSIA – BESSARABIA   Frances Ravden

Serves 2–3   **Preparation 20 mins**   **Standing time 2 hrs**   **Cook 15–20 mins**

Noodle dough   *Filling*
1 egg   **8 oz soft curd cheese (225 g)**
Pinch of salt   **1 tbls top of milk**
4 oz plain flour (115 g)   **Caster sugar to taste**

Beat the egg with a little salt and add enough flour to make a stiff paste. Knead thoroughly, then roll out dough very thinly and leave on a floured board to dry for an hour. Cut into 3″ (7.5 cm) squares. Mix the filling ingredients together and place a teaspoon of cheese mixture on the centre of each square, moisten edges with water and fold over into triangles pressing the edges well together. Leave on the floured board for at least 1 hour. Drop a few at a time into boiling salted water and cook steadily for 15–20 minutes. Drain thoroughly, place on a hot dish and sprinkle with melted butter. Serve with cream cheese.

Traditionally eaten at Shavuot.

Fried Cheese Sambouseks

EGYPT   Doris Afif

Serves 6   **Preparation 20 mins**   **Cook 10 mins**   **Advance**   **Freezable**

1 box matzos   **Oil for frying**
9 eggs   **1½ lb cheese, grated (700 g)**
Salt   **Dried mint to taste**

Mix the grated cheese with 3 beaten eggs, salt and mint until a thick, heavy paste. Add extra eggs if required, then leave mixture to one side. Put water and a teaspoon of salt into a large bowl and then dip each matzo until wet. Remove each matzo and drain, then lay flat on a tea cloth to dry. When matzos are dry but still pliable, cut each into two along the perforations. If the matzo is not pliable then it needs to be soaked again in the water. Then brush each matzo on both sides with beaten egg. Place a tablespoon of the cheese mixture on one end of the matzo and then roll carefully into a cigar shape and seal with brushed egg. Make sure that none of the cheese mixture overflows at the edges. Repeat process for all matzos and then fry them in oil until golden brown. Serve at breakfast, tea or as a snack, either by themselves or with pickled olives or pickled turnips. The sambouseks can be frozen once stuffed and sealed, and then fried directly from frozen (although they may take longer to cook).

A popular dish for Passover.

Topfenknödel – Cheese Dumplings

AUSTRIA

Serves 2–4   **Preparation 10 mins**   **Resting time 30 mins**   **Cook 10–15 mins**

3 oz butter (85 g)   10 oz curd cheese (285 g)
2 eggs   5 oz plain flour (145 g)

Beat butter in mixer until almost white, fold in other ingredients. Let the mixture rest for half an hour. With dampened hands, form the mixture into balls the size of ping-pong balls. Cook in boiling salted water. Serve with melted butter, sugar and cinnamon.

Eggah Bil Badounis – Parsley Omelette

SUDAN   Ruth Synett

Serves 1   **Preparation 5 mins**   **Cook 5 mins**

2 eggs, beaten   3 tbls parsley, chopped
1 tbls onion, chopped   1 tbls breadcrumbs or matzo meal
Salt   Oil for frying

Mix all ingredients together and fry in oil in a shallow pan. Turn over when golden brown and fry on other side. Serve hot or cold.

Eggs Iraqi Style (Pressure-cooked)

IRAQ   Gisele Fattal

Serves 6   **Preparation 15 mins**   **Cook 2 hrs**

6 eggs at room temperature   1 tbls vinegar
Skin of 2 onions   ¼ tsp oil
Pinch of salt

Boil onion skins in water for 10 minutes. Discard the skins and let the liquid cool. Add the vinegar, oil and salt. Arrange the eggs in a pressure cooker and add the onion water. The liquid should more than cover the eggs. Cover and boil until steam rises through vent. Reduce heat and put steam valve on and cook for 2 hours. Let the cooker cool and then open the lid. The eggs should be a golden colour.

This dish is eaten for breakfast on Shabbat with salads, yoghurt, fried slices of aubergine, parsley and pitta bread.

Falafel

ISRAEL/PALESTINE

Makes 150 balls approx   Preparation 25 mins   Standing time 2 hrs   Cook 25 mins
Freezable

1 lb chickpeas, soaked overnight (450 g)
1 large bunch flat-leaf parsley or a mixture
    of parsley and coriander
5 fl oz water (150 ml)
1½–2 scant tbls whole caraway seeds or a
    mixture of caraway and cumin
6 oz onion (150 g)

2 or more green chillies
6 oz flour (150 g)
1 scant tbls salt
Oil for deep frying
1 oz fresh yeast, dissolved in a little water
    (25 g)

Mince (through a coarse blade) the drained chickpeas, onion, parsley and chillies.
Mince the mixture twice if a smoother texture is preferred. It can be successfully
processed in a food processor, but this must be done with care to maintain a coarse
texture. Add remaining ingredients and mix to a soft mass which will hold its shape
when squeezed together. Add more flour if necessary. Leave, covered, in a warm place
for about 2 hours. Then shape into round, flattish 1″ (2.5 cm) patties. Fry the patties in
hot oil until they are a rich, deep golden brown. Drain well and serve hot.
This mixture can be frozen successfully but then it is best to add the minced onion after
defrosting.

Houskovy Knedlik – Savoury Dumpling

CZECHOSLOVAKIA
Nina Orstin

Serves 8   Preparation 15 mins   Cook 30 mins   Advance   Freezable

1 large loaf of white bread, sliced
5 eggs

4 oz butter (115 g)
½ tsp salt

Tear up bread (a few slices at a time) into a large bowl. Melt butter and pour it over
bread. Work it in by hand. Whisk eggs, add salt and pour over bread. Knead mixture
by hand until the consistency of dough. Make a ball (or balls) of whatever size required.
Wrap in silver foil, making parcel as airtight and watertight as possible, and immerse in
boiling water. Boil gently for about 30 minutes. Serve cut into slices. Can be kept in a
refrigerator for up to 24 hours or frozen once cool.

Matzo-Knödel – Dumplings

GERMANY   Odette Dreyfus

Serves 2   **Preparation 5 mins**   **Cook 10–15 mins**

2 matzos, ground   2 eggs
1 onion, finely chopped   1 tbls parsley, finely chopped
Salt and pepper

Mix all ingredients well and form into balls. Place balls in pan of boiling water and cook for 10–15 minutes. The knödels are cooked when they float to the top of the water. Serve in a pre-heated dish and garnish with onion rings fried in oil or butter. Any leftovers can be served the next day by slicing knodles and frying in a shallow pan.

Meat Borekas

EGYPT   Bella Cohen-Setton

Serves 4–6   **Preparation 15 mins**   **Cook 5 mins**

8 oz leftover meat (225 g)   Salt and pepper
1 onion, sliced   4 matzos
1 medium potato, boiled   1 egg for coating
1 egg for mixture   Oil for frying

Fry onion and put through mincer together with meat and potato. Add 1 egg and seasoning and mix well. Soak the matzos and drain. Sandwich meat filling between 2 matzos. Dip in beaten egg and deep-fry until golden brown.

Served at Passover.

Sfongato

GREECE – SALONIKA   Jacqueline Golden

Serves 6   Preparation 10 mins   Gas No 4, 350°F, 185°C   Cook 30 mins approx
                                                           Advance   Freezable

1 lb frozen spinach (450 g)
8 oz low-fat soft cheese (225 g)
Salt and pepper to taste

1 lb mature Cheddar cheese, grated (450 g)
3 beaten eggs
12" (30 cm) ovenproof flan dish, greased

Defrost spinach and squeeze as dry as possible. Combine this with the other ingredients (you can use a mixer for this but not a processor). Turn into flan dish and cook for approximately 30 minutes.

The sfongato is not like a soufflé, it rises a little while cooking but will then be quite flat. It should be eaten warm but can be made in advance and reheated when needed. It can be frozen. It can be served as a starter or as a supper dish with salad. Traditionally, it is served as a first course with a slice of melon.

Variations: Sfongato can be made with finely chopped leeks or grated courgettes which have been quickly cooked in a little butter and then, when cold, squeezed as dry as possible. It can also be made with aubergines which have been baked or grilled until their skins are charred and then the cooked flesh spooned out and chopped.

VEGETABLES

Barley Chulent

POLAND   Rebecca Bonstein

Serves 6–8   Preparation 20 mins   Gas No 3, 325°F, 180°C   Cook 2½–3 hrs

1 lb haricot beans, soaked overnight (450 g)   1 large Spanish onion, chopped
4 oz pearl barley (115 g)   Chicken fat or substitute
Marrow bones   Salt and pepper

Wash and boil barley and then strain to remove starch. Put all ingredients into a large ovenproof pot and cover well with water. Bring to the boil, then put into the oven to cook. Test the beans after 2½ hours since their cooking time does vary.

Brown Butter Beans

ENGLAND   Florence Harris

Preparation 5 mins   Soaking time overnight   Cook 40 mins approx

1 cup butter beans   1 dsp flour
2 tbls brown vinegar   Salt and pepper
Sugar to taste

Soak beans in cold water overnight. Drain. Place in a saucepan, cover with water and boil gently until soft. When soft add the vinegar and sugar. Slake the flour in a little water and add to the beans slowly, stirring all the time until the liquid thickens. Season with salt and pepper to taste.

Viennese-Style Green Beans

AUSTRIA   Connie Grant

Serves 10   **Preparation 15 mins**   **Cook 20 mins**

2 lb 2 oz green beans (1 kg)   3 oz butter or margarine (80 g)
1 onion, finely chopped   3 tbls fresh dill, chopped
1 tbls parsley, chopped   2 oz flour (60 g)
¾ pint stock (425 ml)   ½ tbls sugar
Juice of 1 lemon   Salt and pepper to taste
Sour cream (optional for milk meal)

Cook green beans in salted water until soft and then strain. Fry onion in butter with parsley and dill and then stir in flour and stock. Cook until sauce thickens. Add the green beans to the sauce, then add salt, pepper, sugar and lemon juice and, if for a milk meal, sour cream.

Refried Beans Jewish Style

MEXICO   Sheila Swindon

Serves 4–6   **Preparation 15 mins**   **Cook 20 mins**

1 lb pinti beans, cooked and drained (450 g)   1 tsp chilli powder
3 oz onion, finely chopped (85 g)   7 oz chicken fat/margarine (195 g)
3 oz green peppers, finely chopped (85 g)   Salt to taste
3 garlic cloves, finely chopped

Melt the fat in a large pan, add the onion, pepper, garlic, salt and chilli powder and fry over medium heat for 8–10 minutes. Add the beans and fry for a further 10 minutes stirring occasionally.

Runner Beans

GERMANY   Mrs I. Ryz

Serves 6–8   **Preparation 10 mins**   **Cook 15 mins**

2 lb runner beans, fresh or frozen (900 g)   Beef stock cube
Brine from sweet/sour pickled cucumbers   ½ tsp flour

Bring to the boil sufficient brine to cover the beans and add the stock cube. Mix the flour with a little cold water and add to the brine. Add the runner beans and simmer until tender.

Jaroslav Cabbage

POLAND   Jane Finestone

Serves 6   **Preparation 5 mins**   **Cook 10 mins**

1 white cabbage, finely sliced   1 onion, roughly chopped
2 oz sultanas (55 g)   Dill or caraway seeds
Salt and pepper

Place cabbage in saucepan together with onion, salt and pepper and cover with water. Bring to the boil and simmer, covered, until nearly cooked. Add herbs and sultanas and complete the cooking. Drain well.

Red Cabbage I

GERMANY   Marianne Keats

Preparation 20 mins   **Cook 30 mins**   **Resting time 24 hrs**   **Freezable**

1 medium red cabbage, coarsely chopped   1 large onion, chopped
3 tbls oil for frying   2 tbls malt vinegar
1½ tbls brown or demerara sugar   Salt to taste
1½ tsp caraway seeds   1 large cooking apple, diced

Fry onion in oil until glazed and then add red cabbage and stir well. Add apple and finally all other ingredients. Continue to cook on a low flame, stirring frequently and adding water if mixture becomes dry. This improves after 1–2 days in the refrigerator and also freezes well.

Red Cabbage II

GERMANY   Anne Schwab

Serves 4–6   **Preparation 10 mins**   **Cook 2 hrs**   **Advance**   **Freezable**

1 medium red cabbage, cored and finely   1 tbls water
  sliced   2 tbls grapeseed/sunflower oil
4 fl oz red wine (115 ml)   2 fl oz malt vinegar (55 ml)
2–3 bay leaves   2–3 cooking apples, peeled and chopped
2 tbls sugar   Salt and pepper
1 heaped tsp cornflour

Pour the oil into a large pan and stir in the cabbage until well coated. Add wine, apples, malt vinegar, sugar, salt and pepper and bay leaves. Cover the pan and cook very slowly for approximately 2 hours. When mixture is soft add the cornflour slaked with water and stir until it thickens. This freezes beautifully.

Gogo's Red Cabbage

GERMANY   Patricia Mendelson

Serves 8   **Preparation 15 mins**   **Soak 15 mins**   **Cook 2 hrs**   **Advance**

1 medium to large red cabbage, finely sliced
Red wine
1 large onion, chopped
2–3 Bramley cooking apples, peeled and
 chopped
4 oz brown sugar (115 g)
12 fl oz malt vinegar (340 ml)

4–5 cloves
1 bay leaf
Piece of orange rind
Salt and pepper
2 oz margarine/schmaltz (55 g)
Chestnuts (optional)

Place the cabbage in a large bowl. Pour over ⅓ pint malt vinegar (170 ml) and add boiling water to cover. Leave for 15 minutes. Meanwhile, cook onion gently in some margarine or schmaltz. Add drained cabbage, cloves, bay leaf, orange rind, apples, salt and pepper, brown sugar, remaining malt vinegar and chestnuts if desired. Add enough wine to just cover cabbage. Cover and cook on top of stove for at least an hour, stirring from time to time. If mixture is too runny, allow to boil uncovered for a while. Adjust flavour by adding sugar or vinegar to taste. This improves with re-heating and keeps for 2–3 days.

Chicory

ITALY   Celeste Zarfati

Serves 4   **Preparation 5 mins**   **Gas No 6, 400°F, 200°C**   **Cook 50 mins approx**

2 lb 2 oz chicory (1 kg)
Olive oil

Salt and pepper

Wash the chicory very carefully, keeping it whole. Squeeze out all excess water. Place in an ovenproof dish. Dribble olive oil over the chicory, add salt and pepper and cook in a hot oven. Serve cold.

This dish was traditionally served in Rome on the High Holydays.

Couscous I

LIBYA　　　　　　　　　　　　　　　　　　　　　　　Eveleen Habib

Serves 4–6　　　　　**Preparation 20 mins**　　　　**Cook 1½ hrs approx**

1 lb semolina (450 g)　　　　　　　**Pinch of salt**
2–3 tbls oil

Place semolina in a large bowl and add the salt with the oil. Mix with a spoon to dampen the semolina. Put water in the lower part of a double steamer and when it boils, place semolina in the top. Cover with lid. When it begins to steam, pour 1 glass of cold water, over the semolina. Lower the heat and leave to simmer for 1 hour. Check that there is always water underneath. The lower part of the saucepan can be used to cook soup or a stew, while the couscous is steaming.

After an hour, return semolina to the bowl and allow to cool a little. Pour on 1 glass of water and gently 'work' it with your hands to rid the couscous of any lumps. Return it to the steamer for another 30 minutes. Allow to cool and place on serving plate.

Couscous II

MOROCCO　　　　　　　　　　　　　　　　　　　　Bobbie Barnett

Serves 6　　**Soaking time 12 hrs**　　**Preparation 30 mins**　　**Cook 1 hr**

1 cup of dried chickpeas
3 cups couscous
1 tbls oil
4 carrots, sliced
1 onion, chopped
3 sweet potatoes, peeled and sliced
1 lb red pumpkin, peeled and chopped
　(450 g)
Salt

Garnish
2 small onions, chopped
¼ cup prunes, chopped
¼ cup raisins, chopped
Oil for frying

Soak chickpeas in salted water overnight. Drain. Place chickpeas in a pot. Cover with water, bring to a boil and simmer until almost tender. Add carrots, sweet potato, pumpkin and onion and cook for 20 minutes. While chickpeas and then vegetables are cooking, make the couscous. Soak couscous in cold water for 20 minutes. Line a colander with foil and place it on top of pan containing the vegetables. Put the couscous in the colander and cook for 30 minutes, then put couscous in a dish. Separate grains with a wooden spoon and add approximately 3 tablespoons salted water and 1 tablespoon oil. Return couscous to colander and cook for another 30 minutes. For the garnish, heat oil and sauté onion until brown. To serve, arrange couscous on a large dish and spoon over some of the cooking liquid and the chickpeas. Garnish with the vegetables, fried onions, prunes and raisins.

Kasha I

POLAND   Renee Linder

Cook 30 mins approx

Kasha (buckwheat) as required   **Salted water**

Place buckwheat in a saucepan of boiling salted water so that it is generously covered. Cook until most of the water has evaporated – approximately 30 minutes. Strain if necessary and serve with a main dish. Delicious with gravy. Kasha was also very popular served with milk as a cereal.

Kasha II

POLAND   Greta Goldwater

Serves 4   **Preparation 10 mins**   **Cook 20 mins approx**

1 medium onion, chopped   Fat for frying
1 cup kasha (buckwheat)   2½ cups stock
Salt and pepper   4 oz mushrooms, chopped (optional) (115 g)

Brown onion in fat over a low heat. If using mushrooms, add them to the fat for a minute, then add the buckwheat and cover with the stock. Add seasonings and cook until tender.

Kasha and Varnishkes – Pasta Bows

CANADA   Betty Crystal

Serves 8   **Preparation 10 mins**   **Gas No 4, 350°F, 185°C**   **Cook 45 mins**

1 cup kasha   Oil for frying
1 lb 2 oz pasta bows (500 g)   Salt and pepper
1½ cups boiling water   Chicken/beef gravy (optional)
1 large onion, chopped

Fry onion in plenty of oil until golden brown and reserve. Place kasha in frying pan, add boiling water, cover and cook over a low heat for approximately 15 minutes or until kasha is soft. While kasha is cooking, boil the pasta until *al dente*, rinse and drain well. Return to pan. Add the kasha to the pasta, season with salt and pepper and add onions and oil. Mix well and place in covered casserole and bake in moderate oven. For extra flavour, chicken or beef gravy can be added to mixture.

Marrow Pudding

POLAND   Renee Linder

Serves 6–8   **Preparation 15 mins**   **Gas No 6, 400°F, 200°C**   **Cook 30 mins**

1 medium marrow
Knob of margarine
Salt and pepper

1 large egg
1 tbls fine matzo meal or semolina

Peel and core marrow and cook with very little water until soft. Drain well. Add all ingredients and mash together until the consistency of sponge cake mixture. Put mixture in a greased ovenproof dish and bake in a medium oven. This recipe can be varied by substituting cauliflower for the marrow.

Mofurka – Green Leaf Fry

INDIA

Serves 2–3   **Preparation 15 mins**   **Cook 15 mins**

1 lb fresh spinach, washed (450 g)
1 medium garlic clove, finely chopped
1 medium onion, coarsely chopped
¼ tsp turmeric
½ tsp hot chilli flakes

1 piece fresh ginger, finely chopped
3 tbls vegetable oil
¼ tsp salt
2 large eggs, lightly beaten

Remove tough stems from the washed spinach. Slice leaves into ¾" (2 cm) strips and cook in pan of boiling water for 2 minutes. Remove from the heat and let it stand, covered, for 2 more minutes. Then drain spinach leaves and squeeze them gently to remove as much moisture as possible. Fry onion, garlic and ginger in 2 tablespoons oil for approximately 5 minutes, until lightly browned. Then stir in turmeric, salt and chilli flakes and cook for 2 minutes, stirring all the time. Add the spinach leaves and cook, stirring, for another 2 minutes. In a separate pan cook eggs in the remaining oil until softly scrambled. Fold eggs into the spinach mixture and cook for 1 more minute.

This is served as a breakfast dish in Calcutta.

Savoury Noodle Pudding

CANADA   Betty Crystal

Serves 8–10   **Preparation 15 mins**   **Gas No 6, 400°F, 200°C**   **Cook 1 hr**

12 oz medium or broad noodles (340 g)   ¼ cup oil
1 large onion, coarsely chopped   1 tsp sugar
4 large eggs, beaten   Salt and pepper to taste

Cook noodles and drain well, return to saucepan. Heat oil in an ovenproof baking dish and when hot add the onions and stir well. Return to oven for approximately 5 minutes until onions are lightly browned. Add eggs and seasonings to the noodles and combine well. Stir the noodles into oil and onion mixture and bake uncovered until golden brown.

Aloo-Makala – Fried Potatoes Jewish-Style

INDIA   Thelma Chadourah

Serves 3–4   **Preparation 10 mins**   **Cook 35 mins**

12 small potatoes of similar size, peeled   ¼ tsp turmeric
Salt to taste   Corn oil for frying, to cover potatoes

Boil potatoes with salt and turmeric until almost cooked (take care not to overcook). Drain off water and let potatoes cool. Heat oil in a large saucepan until a high temperature. Drop whole potatoes into oil carefully and cook for 10 minutes or until golden brown. Continue to cook for another 5 minutes and then drain. Serve with meat or chicken.

Potatoes and Artichokes

EGYPT   Bella Cohen-Setton

Serves 4   **Preparation 10 mins**   **Cook 30 mins**

4 artichoke hearts and stalks   Squeeze of lemon juice
4 large potatoes, peeled and cubed   1 tsp flour
Salt and pepper   Chicken stock to cover
1 tsp turmeric powder

Cut artichoke hearts into quarters and place in a pan with the potatoes, sliced artichoke stalks, lemon juice and enough chicken stock to cover. Simmer for 20 minutes. Take 2 tablespoons of artichoke water and mix with the flour, then pour into saucepan and stir in. Continue to simmer for a further 10 minutes. Serve with rice.

Potato Chremslech

BELGIUM Helene Gordon

Serves 4 Preparation 15 mins Cook 35 mins

1½ lb potatoes (675 g)
2 eggs
Salt and pepper

1 oz butter or margarine (30 g)
Medium matzo meal
Oil for frying

Boil potatoes in salted water until tender. Drain and mash with one beaten egg and butter or margarine. Season to taste. Shape into flat cakes, dip into beaten egg and then coat with matzo meal. Shallow fry.

Galushkas

CZECHOSLOVAKIA Naomi Blake

Serves 4 Preparation 15 mins Cook 1½ hrs

3 medium potatoes, grated
Salt and pepper
Flour to bind

1 onion, chopped
Oil for frying

Squeeze excess water from potatoes. Mix potatoes, salt, pepper and flour to form a soft dough. Drop teaspoonfuls of the mixture into boiling salted water. Let them boil for 1 hour and then drain. Fry onion in oil until medium brown, then add the galushkas and fry until golden brown.

Gogo's Kartoffel Klöse

GERMANY Patricia Mendelson

Serves 6–8 Preparation 20 mins Cook 5 mins

2 lb old potatoes (900 g) (cooked day before
 in their skins)
4 oz flour (115 g)
1 egg

Salt
Handful semolina
Small fried croûtons

Peel and grate potatoes, add egg, flour, semolina and salt and make a dough. (You may need a little more flour, depending on the size of the egg.) Roll into a sausage shape and then form into balls, putting a few croûtons into the centre of each one. Cook in boiling salted water until they rise to the surface. Drain.

Latkes

RUSSIA   Mila Greisel

Serves 8–10   **Preparation 15 mins**   **Cook 20 mins**

4 lb potatoes, finely grated (1.8 kg)   4 medium onions, finely chopped
1 tsp baking powder   1 tsp pepper
2 tsp salt   Oil for frying
4 large eggs

Squeeze out all the moisture from the potatoes. Mix all ingredients together and make into small, flat patties. Shallow fry in oil.

Layered Potatoes

HUNGARY   Ilona Grunberger

Serves 6–8   **Preparation 15 mins**   **Gas No 4, 350°F, 185°C**   **Cook 1½ hrs approx**

2 lb 2 oz potatoes (1 kg)   2 oz melted butter (50 g)
1 small onion, chopped   8 fl oz sour cream (225 ml)
6–7 hard boiled eggs, sliced   Salt

Boil the washed potatoes in their skins, peel and slice thinly. Butter a large dish liberally, arrange potatoes and sliced eggs in alternate layers, seasoning with salt and sprinkling chopped onion on top of the eggs. Finish with a layer of potatoes. Pour over melted butter and sour cream. Bake in oven until cooked and top is golden brown.

Resztelt Krumpli – Paprika Potato

HUNGARY   Sandra Berzon

Serves 4   **Preparation 10 mins**   **Cook 30 mins**

1 lb new potatoes (450 g)   2 onions, finely chopped
1 red pepper, finely chopped   1 tomato, chopped
Oil for frying   Paprika to taste

Cook potatoes in their skins in boiling salted water. When cooked, drain, peel and slice. In a separate pan heat some oil and fry onions, red pepper and tomato. When the onions are browned, add paprika powder or paste and stir to make a sauce. Fold in the potato slices and heat through thoroughly. Serve hot.

Potato Preclech

CZECHOSLOVAKIA   Naomi Blake

Serves 3–4   **Preparation 10 mins**   **Cook 10 mins**

1 lb medium potatoes, sliced (450 g)   1 egg
Salt and pepper   Matzo meal to coat
Oil for frying

Dip sliced potatoes in beaten egg and then in matzo meal. Fry in hot oil for a few minutes on each side until golden brown.

Prune and Potato Tzimmes

GERMANY   Minnie Nedas

Serves 4–6   **Soaking time 20 mins**   **Preparation 10 mins**   **Cook 2½ hrs**

1 lb raw prunes (450 g)   4 large potatoes, grated
2 lb boneless brisket (900 g)   ¼ tsp salt
1 onion, sliced   ½ tsp cinnamon
4 tbls schmaltz   ½ cup honey
2 tbls flour   1 cup tzimmes stock
1 pt water (½ litre)

Soak prunes. Seal meat and fry onion in 2 tablspoons of schmaltz in a large saucepan. Add potatoes, prunes and the water. Cook, uncovered, for 1 hour adding more liquid if necessary. Add salt, cinnamon and honey, cover partially and simmer for 1 hour. Brown flour in remaining schmaltz, then stir in a cup of liquid from the meat and cook until it thickens, stirring to make a smooth consistency. Return it to the original pan. Continue to simmer, still stirring, for further 10 minutes.

Migaddarah – Rice with Brown Lentils

SUDAN   Ruth Synett

Serves 4   **Preparation 5 mins**   **Cook 35 mins approx**

½ cup brown lentils   2 onions, sliced
1 cup long grain rice   Salt
Oil for frying   2 oz butter or margarine (55 g)

In a medium-sized saucepan fry the onions in a little oil and when golden remove with a slotted spoon and set aside. Add the lentils to the oil with 2 cups of water and boil until cooked and most of the water has been absorbed. Add the rice and another 2 cups of water. Bring to the boil, cover and then simmer gently until all the water has been absorbed. Just before rice is cooked, add margarine or butter but DO NOT STIR. Serve the rice with the reserved fried onions and a yoghurt and cucumber salad.

Rice with Broad Beans and Dill

IRAN/PERSIA   Sarah Hai

Serves 6–8   **Soaking time 2 hrs**   **Preparation 15 mins**   **Cook 1¼ hrs**

3 tbls oil or margarine
1 large onion, finely sliced
3 tins broad beans
1 cup fresh dill, finely chopped, or 5 tbls
  dill-weed

3½ tbls salt
Pepper
3 cups rice
2 large potatoes

Wash rice three times in lukewarm water. Cover rice with cold water and add 1½ tablespoons of salt and soak for 2 hours. Boil 3 pints water (1½ litres) with 2 tablespoons salt. Pour off cold water from rice. Add rice to boiling water and boil for approximately 5–7 minutes, stir rice once to prevent sticking. Strain the rice and rinse with cold water. Fry onion in oil or margarine until soft. Peel potatoes and cut in slices about ⅓" (1 cm) thick. Put a little oil in a large pan. Cover the bottom of the pan with the sliced potatoes, then put in layers of rice, onion, dill and beans, ending with a layer of rice. Cook on a medium heat for approximately 7 minutes, then put a tea-cloth over the rice, put the lid on and lower the heat and cook for approximately 1 hour. Stir the rice carefully once during cooking and if necessary add a little more seasoning or margarine. When cooked, take the rice out, lifting it carefully, and put the potatoes, which should be nice and golden, around the rice. Serve with roast chicken.

Polo is the Iranian name for rice cooked with other ingredients.

Kitchree – Lentil Rice

INDIA   Berta Shohet

Serves 6   **Soaking time 1 hr**   **Preparation 10 mins**   **Cook 1½ hrs**

2 cups Basmati or long grain rice
1 cup dried red lentils
1 tbls salt
2½ cups water
2–3 tbls tomato paste
2 onions, sliced in rounds

6 oz butter (170 g)
1 tbls oil for frying
Garnish
1 tbls cumin
2–5 cloves garlic, crushed
2 tbls corn oil

Rinse and soak rice for 1 hour and then drain. Rinse and drain red lentils. Brown the onions in the oil and then add water, salt, tomato paste, rice and half the butter. Bring to the boil and then add the red lentils, mixing gently. Bring to the boil again, cover and cook until the liquid has been absorbed. Add the remaining butter and let the mixture simmer over a low heat for 5 minutes. Then mix gently so that the butter and rice are evenly blended. Put a cloth under the lid and let it steam over a very low heat for about 1 hour.

Garnish: Brown the garlic and cumin in the oil. Mix this into the kitchree and serve.

Persian Rice

IRAN/PERSIA   Sarah Hai

Serves 4–6   Soaking time 2 hrs   Preparation 10 mins   Cook 55 mins

2½ cups rice (long grain American or   Salt
    Basmati)   2 tbls oil or butter

Wash rice three times in lukewarm water. Then cover rice with cold water, add 1½ tablespoons of salt and soak for 2 hours. Boil 3 pints water (1½ litres) with 2 tablespoons of salt. Pour off cold water from rice. Add rice to boiling water and boil for 5–7 minutes, stir rice once to prevent sticking. Strain the rice and rinse with cold water. Put oil in a pan, then, taking a spoonful at a time, put the rice evenly into the pot, keeping it away from the sides. Cover with a tea towel and then with the lid. Cook on medium heat for 5 minutes and then lower the heat and cook for approximately 40 minutes. There should be a lovely golden crust at the bottom of the pot. Take the rice out carefully, put it on a large serving dish with pieces of the crust round it.

Chelo is the Iranian name for steamed white rice which is served with various sauces or meat.

Rice and Potato Dish

HOLLAND   Adele Schaverien

Serves 4–6   Preparation 15 mins   Gas No 2, 300°F, 160°C   Cook 1½ hrs

2–3 potatoes, peeled and sliced   8 oz long grain rice, rinsed (225 g)
1 large onion, chopped   Salt and pepper
A little oil

Grease a 10″ × 7″ (25 × 17 cm) ovenproof dish well and cover the bottom with a layer of potatoes. Add a layer of rice and sprinkle with onion, salt and pepper. Repeat layers, finishing with a layer of potatoes placed in an overlapping pattern. Sprinkle with a little onion, salt and pepper. Cover with water and place in the oven. It should be cooked when all the water has been absorbed and the top is crisp and brown. To serve, work a sharp knife around the edge of the dish to loosen before cutting into wedges. Serve with roast meat.

Pelau B'Shejar – Green Squash with Rice

IRAQ

Serves 4–6   Preparation 10 mins   Cook 1¼ hrs

1 cup long grain rice
2 lb green squash (900 g)
1 small onion, chopped
⅛ tsp pepper
½ tsp salt

⅛ tsp turmeric
4 oz butter or margarine (115 g)
1 cup hot water
1 large tomato, chopped, or 1 tbls tomato
    paste

Peel or scrape squash and cut into ½″ (1.5 cm) rounds, or dice. Fry onion in butter together with pepper and turmeric for about 5 minutes or until onion is soft. Add the tomato and fry for a further 5 minutes. Add squash, increasing the heat slightly, and cook for about 20 minutes, stirring occasionally. Add ½ cup of hot water and keep over a medium heat for about 3 minutes. Add the rice and salt and the rest of the water and mix gently to avoid breaking the squash. Cover and cook over a very low heat for 30–40 minutes, until all water is absorbed and rice is tender.

This was often served at Tisha b'Av.

Viennese Sweet and Sour Tomato Kraut

AUSTRIA   Gill Pressburger

Serves 8–10   Preparation 15 mins   Cook 15 mins approx

2 lb white Dutch cabbage, shredded (900 g)
1 large cooking apple, finely chopped
Salt to taste
Pinch of cinnamon
1 tbls cider vinegar

2 tbls tomato purée
1 tbls sugar
1 tbls caraway seeds
1 Spanish onion, sliced
Oil for frying

Sauté onion in oil in large saucepan. Add all other ingredients and water to cover. Simmer until soft.

Tzimmes

POLAND   Rebecca Bonstein

Serves 6   Preparation 20 mins   Refrigerate 30 mins   Cook 45 mins

Tzimmes
1 onion, chopped
1½ lb carrots, diced or sliced (675 g)
1 pint stock or water (½ litre)
1 marrow bone
4 tsp sugar
Salt and pepper
Oil for frying
2 tbls lemon juice
Handful of sultanas

Dumplings
4 oz flour (115 g)
1½ oz chicken fat or margarine (45 g)
1 egg, beaten
Salt and pepper
Water to bind

Dumplings: Mix together flour, salt and pepper with the fat until the mixture is like fine crumbs. Add the egg and enough water to make a loose, pliable dough. Leave in fridge for 30 minutes. With wet or floured hands roll into small balls and add to the tzimmes. Heat oil in a large heavy-bottomed pan. Add onions and carrots and fry until onions are translucent. Add all other ingredients, cover and cook on a low heat for approximately 45 minutes.

Tzimmes with Chestnuts

HUNGARY   Vera Grodzinski

Serves 4   Preparation 15 mins   Cook 25–30 mins   Advance

1 lb carrots, sliced (450 g)
8 oz chestnuts, peeled and quartered (225 g)
1 tbls honey or more, according to taste
2 tbls oil/margarine
Salt

Glaze carrots slowly in oil or margarine. Add chestnuts and then honey. Simmer until carrots are soft but crunchy. Add a little water if necessary. Cook gently to prevent burning.

This recipe was used for Rosh Hashana as the new season's chestnuts came to the market in Hungary/Romania in September. A popular dish, it could be used to make a required 'Shechechayanu' over the chestnuts.

Vegetable Pulav

INDIA   Edwina Slotover

Serves 4–6   **Preparation 15 mins**   **Cook 30 mins approx**

2 medium onions, minced
1″ piece root ginger, finely chopped (2.5 cm)
4 cloves of garlic, crushed
2 tbls oil
1 green chilli, finely chopped
1 bunch coriander leaves, coarsely chopped

3 medium carrots, diced
8 oz fresh peas (225 g)
2 tomatoes, skinned and chopped
¼ tsp turmeric
Salt and pepper
1 cup rice

Sauté onions in the oil. Add ginger, garlic and chilli and cook for 2–3 minutes. Then add carrots and peas, turmeric, salt and pepper. Stir well. Add a cupful of water. Cover and allow to simmer until the vegetables are cooked but still crisp. Add tomatoes and adjust seasonings. Cook until the juices have almost evaporated. In a separate saucepan cook the rice until almost ready, then stir the vegetable mixture into the rice. Add coriander leaves, stir well and return to a low heat until the rice is fully cooked.

Served for Friday night dinner in Bombay.

SALADS

Chatzilim Mizrachyim – 'Oriental' Aubergine
ISRAEL/PALESTINE

Serves 6–8   Preparation 30 mins   Gas No ¼, 230°F, 110°C   Cook 15 mins
                                              Marinate 30 mins minimum

2 lb large aubergines (1 kg)
1 lb peppers of mixed colours (450 g)
Hot red or green chillies, to taste, sliced
1 cup vinegar (cider or wine)

10–12 cloves garlic, sliced in thin slivers
1–2 tbls good honey
⅓–½ cup olive oil

Slice the unpeeled aubergines lengthwise into ⅓″ (1 cm) thick slices. Salt lightly and leave for about 30 minutes in a very low oven.

To prepare the peppers, char them on an open fire or grill. Put the charred peppers in a bowl and cover them with a cloth or seal for 10 minutes in a plastic bag. Then peel, remove seeds and rinse well. Slice into wide strips.

Either fry, grill or barbecue the aubergines. Mix with the peppers and cover with a cloth to keep warm. Melt honey with olive oil in a small frying pan. Add vinegar and salt and bring to a rapid boil. Then add garlic (either raw for a strong flavour or lightly fried in oil for a milder flavour) and sliced chillies. Boil on a very high heat for a few minutes, until the liquid looks glossy and starts to thicken. Pour over the vegetables. Adjust salt to taste. Allow to marinate for a few hours. For a less 'pickled' salad allow to stand for 30 minutes only. The salad can be eaten either warm or cold.

Jaroslav Cucumber – Sweet and Sour Cucumber Salad
POLAND   Jane Finestone

Serves 4–6   Preparation 10 mins   Standing time 1 hr

1 cucumber, peeled and thinly sliced
2 tbls malt vinegar

1 dsp salt
2 tbls sugar

Place cucumber in a bowl and sprinkle with salt. Cover with foil or plate and weigh down with weights or tins for half to 1 hour. From time to time pour off water and turn slices. Mix together vinegar and sugar and add to cucumber. Chill for 1 hour and serve with cold meats or fish.

Cucumber Salad

CZECHOSLOVAKIA   Jackie Gryn

Serves 6–8   **Preparation 10 mins**   **Standing time 1 hr**

2 cucumbers, peeled and thinly sliced	White malt vinegar
1 tbls sugar	Salt and white pepper
Paprika	Dill

Sprinkle cucumber with salt and drain in a colander for 1 hour. Place slices in a shallow dish and cover with vinegar mixed with water to taste. Then add sugar, white pepper, dill and paprika to taste. Taste for sourness after 1 hour.

Kraut Salat – White Cabbage Salad

GERMANY   Susan Straus

Preparation 15 mins   **Rest 4 hrs**   **Advance**

3 lb white cabbage, finely shredded	*Dressing*
Salt	2 tbls citric acid
Handful of parsley, chopped	6 tbls water from cabbage
	2 tbls mayonnaise
	A little oil
	White pepper

Place cabbage in a bowl and sprinkle with salt. After a short while, squeeze the liquid from the cabbage. Retain the liquid for use in the dressing. Add parsley to cabbage. Mix dressing ingredients together. Pour over cabbage and stir thoroughly. The salad is best when prepared a few hours in advance.

Wiener Kartoffel Salat – Viennese Potato Salad

AUSTRIA   Suzy Landes

Serves 4   **Preparation 5 mins**   **Cook 20 mins**

2 lb small new potatoes (900 g)	*Dressing*
2 spring onions, chopped	1 tbls Dijon mustard
	1 tbls acetic acid
	1 tbls sugar
	Oil
	Salt and pepper to taste

Boil potatoes in their skins until soft. Meanwhile put mustard into a basin, add sugar, salt, pepper and acetic acid. When blended, add oil gradually until mixture is as thick as mayonnaise. Add water to thin. Finally add the spring onions and pour over hot potatoes.

Ensalada de Pimientos Rojos

SPAIN   Patricia Ward

Serves 6   **Preparation 15 mins**   **Gas No 6, 400°F, 200°C**   **Cook 30 mins**
                                                                      Refrigerate 2 hrs   Advance

2¼ lb red peppers (1 kg)   1 large beefsteak tomato
2–3 large cloves garlic   Coarse sea salt
4 tbls olive oil   2 tbls wine vinegar

Bake whole peppers, unskinned, with the garlic and tomato in a large baking tin for 30 minutes, turning peppers after 15 minutes. Remove tomato skin and chop flesh and skin and slice peppers, reserving any juices. Make a dressing by skinning and crushing garlic and mixing with tomato. Add the oil, vinegar and reserved juices and salt to taste. Mix thoroughly. Arrange the peppers on a serving dish and pour over the dressing. Refrigerate.

Mixed Pepper Salad

ROMANIA   The Yager Family

Serves 6   **Preparation 40 mins**   **Cook 20 mins**   **Advance**

2 green peppers   2 bay leaves
2 red peppers   1 pint malt vinegar (565 ml)
2 yellow peppers   6 fl oz water (175 ml)
¾ oz pickling spices (20 g)

Singe skins of peppers and peel under cold water, then cut into slices. Boil vinegar, water, spices and bay leaves for 3 minutes, pour over the peppers and leave until cold. Refrigerate for at least 24 hours.

Tabbuleh – Cracked Wheat Salad

IRAQ   Linda Yentob

Serves 4   **Soaking time 30 mins**   **Preparation 5 mins**   **Advance**

¼ cup fine cracked wheat (Bulgur)   1 tbls olive oil
1 cup broad leaf parsley, finely chopped   Salt and pepper to taste
1 large tomato, seeded and chopped   ¼ cup spring onions, white part only,
½ cup lemon juice   chopped

Rinse the wheat and soak for 30 minutes, drain and squeeze out water. Mix in parsley, spring onions and tomato. Add wheat, oil, lemon juice, salt and pepper and mix well.

Shalram – Pickled Turnip

IRAQ Yvonne Cohen

Preparation 15 mins   **Resting time 3 days**   **Advance**

2 lb turnips (900 g)
1 beetroot, peeled and cut into small pieces
½ pint vinegar (280 ml)

Several garlic cloves
1½ pints water (850 ml)
3 oz salt (85 g)

Wash turnips well and cut off a slice from tops and bottoms. Cut lengthwise into quarters. Place in glass jar with beetroot. Cover with the pickling solution prepared from remaining ingredients. Keep in a warm place for about three days.

Yoghurt and Cucumber Salad

SUDAN Ruth Synett

Serves 4   **Preparation 5 mins**

1 small carton yoghurt
Fresh or dried mint to taste

½ cucumber, finely chopped
Salt and black pepper

Mix all ingredients well, seasoning to taste.

DESSERTS

Apple Pudding

AUSTRIA   Ilse Schwarzmann

Serves 8–10   Preparation 15 mins   Cook 1 hr approx   Gas No 4, 350°F, 185°C
Freezable

6 apples, peeled and sliced   3 oz butter (80 g)
½ cup milk   ¼ cup sugar
1 cup flour   1 egg
1 tsp baking powder   Few drops vanilla essence

Stew apples in a little sugar and water. Cream butter and sugar. Add egg, milk and flour. Then add vanilla essence and baking powder. Grease an ovenproof dish and put stewed apples into dish, pour batter on top. Bake for approximately 1 hour until sponge is cooked. Serve with cream or hot custard.

Apple Strudel

POLAND   Sally Bloom

Serves 16   Preparation 20 mins   Resting time 30 mins   Gas No 4, 350°F, 185°C
Cook 1 hr   Advance   Freezable

Pastry   *Filling*
1 lb flour (450 g)   3½ lb cooking apples, thinly sliced (1.6 kg)
8 oz margarine (225 g)   Raisins
2 eggs   Brown sugar
8 oz sugar (225 g)   Cinnamon
                                     Marmalade
Baking tin 11″ × 9″ (28 cm × 23 cm) Oil

Make pastry by rubbing fat into flour, then adding sugar and eggs. Chill in fridge for 30 minutes. Oil baking tin and put thin layer of pastry on the bottom and round the sides. Spread with thin layer of marmalade (this layer only). Place some of the apple slices on top and sprinkle with raisins, sugar and cinnamon. Cover with a thin layer of pastry and brush with oil. Repeat layers as before, finishing with the pastry. Sprinkle top with mixture of sugar and cinnamon. Bake for at least 1 hour.

Apricot and Almond Slices

AUSTRIA   Jean Rosenberg

Preparation 20 mins   Gas No 5, 375°F, 190°C   Cook 30 mins   Advance   Freezable

Pastry
4 oz margarine (100 g)
4 oz potato flour (100 g)
1 egg
3 oz caster sugar (80 g)
4 oz fine matzo meal (100 g)

2 Swiss roll tins, greased

Filling
1 lb dried apricots, soaked in hot water
  (450 g)
2 egg whites
3 oz ground almonds (80 g)
4 oz caster sugar (100 g)
Apricot jam (or dark red jam)
Flaked almonds
Almond essence or vanilla sugar

Rub margarine into potato flour and matzo meal. Stir in sugar and egg and make into pastry. Line Swiss roll tins with pastry. Cover pastry with apricot jam and then with the halved apricots. Beat 2 egg whites until they form peaks, add caster sugar and beat again. Stir in ground almonds and almond essence or vanilla sugar. Pipe this mixture in a trellis pattern over pastry and topping and then sprinkle with flaked almonds. Bake. When cool, cut into squares and serve.

Traditionally served at Pesach.

Aros Di Leci – Rice with Milk

YUGOSLAVIA   Bulka Danon

Serves 4–6   Preparation 5 mins   Cook 30 mins   Advance

½ tea-cup ground rice
¾ pint milk (½ litre)

2 tbls sugar
Cinnamon or grated chocolate

Place ground rice, milk and sugar in a saucepan and heat for 30 minutes, stirring occasionally, until the mixture is very thick. Pour into small dishes and allow to cool. Decorate with cinnamon or grated chocolate, forming a pattern or Jewish symbol.

Baklava

IRAN/PERSIA   Maryam Zenoubian

Makes 12   Preparation 50 mins   Gas No 4, 350°F, 185°C   Cook 25 mins   Advance

¾ cup blanched almonds
¾ cup shelled pistachios
½ cup granulated sugar
1 tsp ground cardamom
4 oz unsalted butter, melted (115 g)
1 lb pack frozen filo pastry (450 g)

13″ (30 cm) Swiss roll tin, greased

Syrup
1½ cups sugar
½ cup rosewater
1 cup water

Garnish
2 tbls ground pistachios

Grind almonds and pistachios together, then combine with sugar and cardamom and mix well. Cut filo pastry to fit the baking tin. Place 1 layer of pastry on the bottom of the tin. Brush with melted butter. Repeat twice and then evenly sprinkle 3 tablespoons of the nut mixture on top. Continue building up layers in the same way finishing with 3 layers of pastry on top. Place tin in pre-heated oven and bake until brown.
Syrup: Boil sugar and water in pan over medium heat for 15 minutes. Add rosewater and set aside.
Remove tin from oven and pour syrup over baklava. Decorate with pistachio nuts.

Beaconsfield Pudding

ENGLAND

Serves 4–6   Preparation 15 mins   Cook 2 hrs approx

4 oz treacle or golden syrup (115 g)
4 oz flour (115 g)
2 oz demerara sugar (55 g)
2oz suet, finely chopped (55 g)
½ tsp ground ginger

½ tsp allspice
2 eggs
½ tsp powdered cinnamon
½ tsp bicarbonate of soda

Warm treacle, sift flour into it and then add sugar, suet and spices. Beat the eggs well and dissolve the bicarbonate of soda in a little water. Mix all thoroughly together and pour into a well-greased mould. Cover with greaseproof paper which has been pleated to allow the pudding to expand and tie with string. Steam for at least 2 hours. Turn out and serve hot.

Tvarohovy Knedliky – Cheese Dumplings

CZECHOSLOVAKIA

Hana Rayner

Serves 8   **Preparation 10 mins**   **Standing time 2 hrs**   **Cook 10 mins**

1 oz margarine/oil mixed (25 g)
8 oz curd cheese (225 g)
Pinch salt
3 eggs, separated

3 oz fine semolina (85 g)
To serve
Melted butter, sugar and cinnamon

Cream fat and add egg yolks one at a time. Add salt and then egg whites, whisking fast. Slowly add cheese, then, a little faster, semolina. Let the mixture stand for a minimum of 2 hours. Drop dessertspoonfuls of the mixture into lightly salted water and simmer, covered, for 10 minutes. Drain.
To serve: Drizzle a little melted butter over dumplings and then sprinkle with sugar and cinnamon mixture. Can also be served with grated or crumbled honey cake or plum compote.

Cheese Blintzes

RUSSIA – BESSARABIA

Frances Ravden

Serves 4   **Preparation 5 mins**   **Cook 10 mins**   **Advance**   **Freezable**

4 oz flour (115 g)
¼ pint milk (140 ml)
8 oz soft curd cheese (225 g)
Grated lemon rind to taste
1 egg

¼ pint water (140 ml)
Sugar
Salt and pepper
To serve
Sour cream

Add a little salt, pepper, grated lemon rind and sugar to the cheese. Make a smooth batter with the egg, flour, milk and water, adding salt to taste. Grease a heated frying pan and pour in about 3 tablespoonfuls of the batter – just sufficient to cover the bottom of the pan with a very thin layer. Cook over a moderate heat until the pancake is firm, frying on one side only, then invert onto a clean cloth. Place a tablespoonful of the cheese mixture in the centre and fold over to form triangle. Continue with the remaining batter and filling. Then place blintzes back in the frying pan and fry lightly on both sides until golden brown. Serve with sour cream.

Chestnut Roll (or Balls)

HUNGARY   Aniko Grunsfeld

Preparation 20 mins   **Cook 20 mins**

1 lb cooked chestnuts (450 g) or chestnut
   purée
4 oz margarine (115 g)
8 oz icing sugar (225 g)

Rum or rum essence (optional)
4 oz melted chocolate (115 g)
To serve
Fresh cream

If using fresh chestnuts, cook, remove skins, mash well and sieve. Process in a food processor with remaining ingredients until mixture is smooth. Form into a roll or small balls. Cover in melted chocolate. Slice roll and serve with fresh cream. The chestnut balls can be served with tea.

Compote

GERMANY

Serves 6   Preparation 5 mins   Soaking time 2 hrs   Cook 20 mins   Advance

4 oz dried apricots (115 g)
4 oz figs (115 g)
4 oz prunes (115 g)
4 oz apple rings (115 g)

1 tsp cinnamon or 1 cinnamon stick
Large slice of lemon rind
Sugar to taste

Rinse fruit in cold water and then soak in fresh water for at least 2 hours. Cook in the soaking water, with remaining ingredients, on a low heat for 15–20 minutes. Serve warm or cold.

Audrey's Date Dessert

SOUTH AFRICA

Preparation 20 mins   **Gas No 4, 350°F, 185°C**   **Cook 40–50 mins**

8 oz cooking dates, chopped (225 g)
2 tbls butter, cubed
1 egg, beaten
½ tsp mixed spice
1–2 tbls ginger, chopped (optional)
1 tsp lemon rind, grated

8″ (20 cm) ovenproof dish, greased

2 cups freshly made tea
1¼ cups S.R. flour
1½ cups brown sugar

Sauce
4 tbls golden syrup
1 tbls boiling water

Sift together flour and mixed spice and add half a cup of brown sugar. Add lemon rind and butter to the dates, with the ginger if desired. Pour over 1 cup of hot tea and stir until butter is dissolved. Add egg to the flour mixture and mix well. Stir in date mixture. Spoon into a dish and sprinkle with remaining sugar and then pour over second cup of hot tea. Bake. Serve with sauce made by heating together golden syrup and water.

Fruit Pudding

GERMANY   Mrs I. Ryz

Serves 8   Preparation 20 mins   Gas No 4, 350°F, 185°C   Cook 45 mins   Advance

2 lb plums (not sweet), diced (900 g)
2 lb apples, diced (900 g)
1 lb sultanas (450 g)
1 lb flour (450 g)

2 eggs
3 tbls sugar
¾ cup oil

Mix the flour with the eggs to make a dough, adding a little water if necessary. Roll out fairly thinly. Cover the bottom of a well-greased baking tin with a layer of dough. Mix the fruit together and put a layer of fruit onto the base layer of dough. Sprinkle with sugar. Repeat the layers until all the fruit is used up, finishing with a layer of dough. Pour the oil over the pudding and bake, covered with foil, in a preheated oven. After 25 minutes remove foil and allow pudding to brown.

Halva

IRAN/PERSIA   Maryam Zenoubian

Preparation 25 mins　　　　　　　**Cook 30 mins**　　　　　**Advance**

1 cup butter	½ tsp saffron dissolved in ¼ cup hot water
2 cups flour	¼ cup rose water
⅓ cup water	½ tsp ground cardamom
1 cup sugar	2 tbls ground pistachios

Melt butter in a large skillet, add flour gradually, stirring constantly with a wooden spoon. Fry over medium heat for 20 minutes until golden brown. Remove from heat. Bring water and sugar to boil in a saucepan, remove from heat and add saffron, rose water and cardamom. Mix well. Slowly add to warm flour/butter mixture, stirring constantly to make a thick, smooth paste.
Transfer to a flat plate and pat firmly with a spoon. Decorate by making geometric patterns with a spoon. Garnish with pistachio nuts. Chill. Cut into small pieces and serve cold as a main dish with bread, or as a dessert.

Jacob Pudding

RUSSIA   Gun Wood

Serves 2–3　　**Preparation 5 mins**　　**Standing time 1 hr**　　**Gas No 3, 325°F, 180°C**
Cook 40 mins

4 oz jam or marmalade (115 g)	3 or 4 slices buttered bread
2 large eggs	1 pint milk (570 ml)
Pinch of salt	

Cut bread into fingers, spread them thickly with jam or marmalade and place them lattice-fashion in a buttered pie dish. Beat the eggs well, add a pinch of salt and the milk and pour slowly over the bread. Cover and let the dish stand for at least 1 hour, then bake in a moderate oven.

Kaiserschmarren – Broken Pancakes

AUSTRIA   Annette Saville

Serves 2   **Preparation 5 mins**   **Resting time 20 mins**   **Cook 10 mins**

½ lb flour (225 g)   1 large egg
¼ lb raisins (115 g)   Oil for frying
Sugar   Caster sugar for sprinkling
½ pint milk (or water if preferred) (285 ml)

Make batter with flour, egg and milk. Add raisins (washed) and sugar to taste. Let batter rest for 20 minutes. Heat oil and make pancakes. Fry on both sides (or place under grill for second side). Take 2 forks and tear up pancakes. Sprinkle with caster sugar. Serve with stewed plums or prunes.

Emperor Franz Joseph stopped for lunch at an inn in Austria. The girl in the kitchen was distressed because she broke a pancake cooked for him. The owner of the inn tore the pancake up with forks. Thereafter the dish was called Kaiserschmarren (Emperor's Trifle).

Citronen Creme – Lemon Cream I

GERMANY   Patricia Mendelson

Serves 3   **Preparation 10–15 mins**   **Refrigerate 2 hrs**   **Advance**

3 eggs, separated   Rind and juice of 2 lemons
4 oz sugar (115 g)

Add sugar to egg yolks. Stir very well. Add lemon rind and juice and stir over a bain-marie until mixture thickens. Cool. Beat egg whites stiffly, fold into egg yolk mixture and refrigerate.

Lemon Cream II

GERMANY   Anne Schwab

Serves 6   **Preparation 5 mins**   **Cook 10 mins**   **Refrigerate 4 hrs**   **Advance**

3 eggs, separated   Grated rind of 1 lemon
3 tbls sugar   Juice of 2 lemons
8 fl oz orange juice (225 ml)   16 fl oz water (455 ml)
6–7 tsp cornflour, slaked in water

Mix egg yolks with sugar. Stir in lemon rind and juice, then orange juice and water. Pour mixture into a saucepan and bring to the boil stirring continuously. Remove from heat. Stir in cornflour mixture and bring to the boil again, stirring constantly until it thickens. Remove from heat. When almost cool, fold in stiffly beaten egg whites. Refrigerate.

Florida Key Lime Pie

USA   Phyllis Kilstock

Serves 6–8   Preparation 15 mins   Gas No 4, 350°F, 185°C   Cook 15 mins

1 tin condensed milk
½ cup lime juice
½ tsp cream of tartar

4 eggs, separated
6 tbls sugar
9″ (23 cm) cooked pastry shell

Mix condensed milk, egg yolks and lime juice. Fold in one stiffly beaten egg white. Pour into pie shell. Beat the remaining three egg whites stiffly and gradually add the sugar and cream of tartar. Pile on top of lime mixture and cook until golden brown.

Lockshen Cheese Dessert

SOUTH AFRICA

Serves 6–8   Preparation 10 mins   Gas No 2, 300°F, 160°C   Cook 1 hr

1 packet thick egg lockshen, cooked and
   strained
1 lb cream cheese (450 g)
5 fl oz single cream (140 ml)
4 oz butter, melted (115 g)

3 eggs
½ cup sultanas (optional)
8 tbls sugar
Dabs of butter
Cinnamon and sugar mixture to sprinkle

Mix all ingredients with lockshen and put into dish. Put dabs of butter on top and then sprinkle with plenty of cinnamon and sugar. Cook in a buttered ovenproof dish.

Matzo Cake

YUGOSLAVIA   Henake Konforte

Serves 4   Preparation 20 mins   Cook 12 mins

4 matzos
4 eggs, separated

11 oz sugar (300 g)
15 fl oz water (½ litre)

Break matzos into small pieces and soak in cold water for 10 minutes. Drain well. Beat egg whites until stiff, add the beaten yolks and matzo and gently mix together. Deep-fry tablespoons of the mixture in very hot oil. When cooked, drain and place in serving dish. Meanwhile, boil the sugar with the water for about 10 minutes and then pour over the matzo balls.

Traditionally served at Pesach.

Fine Matzo Loksh

CZECHOSLOVAKIA   Ruth Arnold

Serves 10   Preparation 15 mins   Gas No 4, 350°F, 185°C   Cook 45 mins approx

8 matzos
7 oz sugar (200 g)
Juice and grated rinds of 1 lemon and
    1 orange
3½ oz ground almonds/nuts (100 g)
2 glasses wine

10 eggs, lightly beaten
Pinch of salt
1 apple, grated
½ tsp cinnamon
2 tbls melted margarine
1 tbls medium matzo meal

Soak the matzos in water and squeeze out. Place in a large bowl and add all other ingredients. Mix thoroughly. Place in a well-greased ovenproof dish and cook until golden brown. Serve hot.

Iraqi Melfoof

IRAQ

Preparation 20 mins   Gas No 6, 400°F, 200°C   Cook 8–9 mins

3 cups almonds or almonds combined with
    walnuts or pistachios
2 tbls rose water or more (the mixture
    should be a little moist)

1 cup caster sugar
1 tbls ground cardamom
1 packet filo pastry
A little oil

Blanch and grind almonds. Mix almonds, sugar, cardamom and rose water. Cut sheets of pastry into rectangles 10″ × 5″ (25 × 12½ cm). Brush top surfaces with oil and cover with a damp cloth (if not kept moist they tend to crumble when folded). Using one rectangle at a time, place 1 dessertspoon of the almond mixture in the centre of the rectangle, slightly fold over the longer sides and roll up, starting from a short side. Repeat with remaining pastry and bake in a preheated oven. Cool and keep in covered container in fridge or freezer.

Noodle Pudding

GERMANY   Ruth Knoller

Serves 6–8   Preparation 15 mins   Gas No 4, 350°F, 185°C   Cook 45 mins approx

8 oz vermicelli (225 g)
2 tsp butter
Sugar to taste
Handful of raisins or sultanas
1 tbls candied peel, chopped

8–9 fl oz milk (225–250 ml)
3 eggs, separated
2 apples, peeled and finely sliced
1 tbls nuts

Cook vermicelli as packet instructions. Cream butter and sugar, add egg yolks and beat well. Add milk, drained vermicelli, apples, dried fruit, nuts and peel. Stir well. Whisk egg whites and fold into mixture. Bake in a greased ovenproof dish.

Orange Salad

HOLLAND   Adele Schaverien

Preparation 30 mins   **Advance**

1 orange per person
Water

Sugar
Orange liqueur (optional)

Make enough sugar syrup for the required number of oranges by steadily boiling 1 part sugar to 3 parts water (using more sugar if a heavier syrup is desired) until thickened. Leave to cool. Place oranges in a bowl and pour boiling water over them and leave for a few moments – this makes it easier to remove peel. Peel the oranges in a circular movement (a sawing action with a sharp knife is best), then with the point of the knife, prise the segments away from the membrane. Place the orange sections in a serving dish and pour over the cooled syrup. This dish can be improved by adding orange liqueur such as Cointreau or Curaçao to the cooled syrup.

This dish is of English/Dutch/Spanish origin.

Palacsinken – Pancakes

AUSTRIA Erika Crocker

Preparation 20 mins **Cook 20 mins** **Advance**

2 oz butter, softened (55 g)
2 oz caster sugar (55 g)
5 tbls flour
1 pint milk (570 ml)
3 eggs, separated
½ tsp vanilla essence

Oil for cooking
Ground almonds to taste
Caster sugar to sprinkle
To serve
Whipped cream

Beat milk, flour, butter, egg yolks, sugar and vanilla until blended. Whisk whites and fold into mixture. Heat oil in frying pan and pour in enough batter for 1 thick pancake. Cook slowly on one side only until the surface bubbles. Put on plate. Sprinkle with sugar and ground almonds. Repeat this process until all batter is used up, stacking pancakes in a pancake 'cake'. Reheat if necessary and serve in small wedges with whipped cream.

Palacsinta – Pancakes

HUNGARY Sandra Berzon

Serves 6 **Preparation 10 mins** **Cook 2 mins**

2 heaped tbls flour
2 eggs, beaten
1 cup fizzy soda/lemonade
½ pint milk (285 ml)

2 tsp sugar
Oil for frying
To serve
Chopped nuts, sugar, jam

Mix the flour, eggs, milk and sugar in a bowl and add soda or lemonade. Heat a little oil or butter in a frying pan until very hot, then pour in a little of the batter. When cooked on one side, toss to cook the other side. Fill with nuts and jam, fold and sprinkle with sugar.

Pashka

RUSSIA

Preparation 20 mins   **Refrigerate 24 hrs**   Advance

2 lb cottage cheese (900 g)   ½ lb butter, softened (225 g)
½ cup sour cream   1 scant cup sugar
½ cup chopped fruit or raisins   ½ cup chopped almonds
1 egg, beaten

Force cottage cheese through a strainer, add butter and sour cream. Mix well. Add sugar and egg and beat until smooth. Mix in almonds and fruit. Line a bowl (preferably wooden) with muslin or kitchen paper, pour in mixture and cover with kitchen paper. Put a weight on the top and keep under press in refrigerator for 24 hours. Turn out onto a plate and serve.

Pavlova

AUSTRALIA   Goldie Selig

Preparation 15 mins   **Gas No 9, 475°F, 250°C**   **Cook 1 hr**   Advance

8 egg whites   16 tbls caster sugar
½ tsp salt   1 heaped tbls cornflour
1 small tbls white vinegar

Grease an ovenproof glass dish or pizza pan and cover with bakewell paper (or, which is better, a brown paper bag which has been rinsed with water and then squeezed out to remove excess water). Beat the egg whites with salt in mixer until they are stiff. Gradually add the sugar, beating until the sugar is absorbed and the mixture stands in stiff peaks. Mix in cornflour and vinegar and then spoon pavlova into prepared dish. Place in preheated oven, turning down the oven *immediately* to Gas No ¼, 225°F, 125°C and cook for about 1 hour. Turn out onto a platter with the hard side down. When cool decorate with whipped cream and seasonal fruits. A typical selection in Australia would be strawberries, passion fruit and bananas, dipped in lemon juice to prevent discolouration.

Rødgrød Med Fløde – Red Fruit Jelly with Cream

DENMARK   Birtha Tager

Serves 6   **Preparation 15 mins**   **Cook 15 mins**   **Advance**

1½ lb mixed soft fruit: redcurrants
  raspberries, blackcurrants, etc. (700 g)
8 oz sugar (225 g)

1–2 tbls potato flour/arrowroot to each pint
  (550 ml) of fruit juice
1 oz almonds (30 g)
To serve
Cream

Wash the fruit in cold water. Place it in a large pan with just enough cold water to cover. Simmer for 15 minutes until soft. Sieve the fruit. Measure juice and weigh out potato flour or arrowroot. Dissolve sugar in the juice over a gentle heat. Remove from heat. Slake the potato flour or arrowroot with a little water and stir it into the juice. Return to the heat and simmer, stirring constantly until clear. Do *not* bring to the boil. The mixture should resemble a syrup. Pour into a glass bowl or individual serving dishes and sprinkle a little sugar over the top to prevent a skin forming. Decorate with almonds and serve with cream.

This dish was often served on Shabbat with a milk meal.

Strawberry Bavarian Cream

AUSTRIA   Ilse Schwarzman

Serves 8   **Preparation 20 mins**   **Advance**

1 large packet sponge fingers
1 lb strawberries, cleaned and sieved (450 g)
1 packet strawberry jelly

1 pint boiling water (½ litre)
½ pint whipping cream (285 ml)

Dissolve jelly in boiling water. Line a dish with sponge fingers and pour a little jelly over them. Allow rest of the jelly to cool, but not set. Fold sieved strawberries into jelly. Whip cream and fold into jelly mixture. Pour into dish and allow to set.

Sutlach – Milk Pudding

GREECE

Serves 6   **Preparation 15 mins**   **Cook 5 mins**

2½ cups milk
1½ cups fine semolina
1–2 tsp orange rind, finely grated

3 tbls rice flour
¼ cup sugar

Mix rice flour and semolina together in a large bowl. Slowly add 2 tablespoons of milk while stirring, either with your hand or a wooden spoon, to mix the milk smoothly into the dry ingredients. Then add just enough milk to form a thick, smooth liquid. In a large pan, heat the remaining milk with the sugar until sugar dissolves. Remove from the heat and pour the liquid very slowly into the semolina mixture, stirring constantly. When all the milk has been added return the mixture to the saucepan and bring to a gentle simmer. Stir constantly until the mixture begins to thicken. Add the orange rind and pour into small bowls to cool.

Variations: Rose water may be substituted for the orange peel. The Jews in Rhodes use cinnamon to flavour and substitute ground almonds for the semolina.

Waffles for Pesach

SWITZERLAND   Lys Kenley

Serves 8–10   **Preparation 10 mins**   **Cook 20 mins**

9 oz butter (250 g)
12 dsp caster sugar

12 eggs, separated
12 dsp fine matzo meal

Beat egg whites until stiff and reserve. Beat butter, sugar and egg yolks well. Mix in matzo meal, then fold in the egg whites. Spoon the mixture into a hot waffle pan and cook until golden.

Traditionally served at Pesach.

BREADS AND BISCUITS

Breads

Homemade Bagels

USA   Betty Crystal

Makes 12   **Preparation 20 mins**   **Proving time 35 mins**   **Gas No 5, 375°F, 190°C**
Cook 30–35 mins

1½ cups warm water
2 tbls sugar
1 tbls salt

1 packet active dry yeast or 1 cake
compressed yeast
4½ cups (approx) unsifted flour

Rinse a large bowl under hot water to warm it. Pour in the warm water. Sprinkle or crumble yeast on top of water and stir until dissolved. Stir in sugar, salt and 4 cups of flour to make a soft dough. Turn out onto a lightly floured board and knead for about 10 minutes, adding flour to board as needed, until dough is smooth and elastic. Place in a greased bowl and turn once to grease the top of the dough. Cover bowl with a cloth and set in a warm place to rise for 15 minutes. Then punch down dough and roll on a lightly floured board into a 9″ × 5″ (22.5 cm × 12.5 cm) rectangle about 1″ (2.5 cm) thick. Cut into 12 equal strips with a floured knife. Roll each strip into a ½″ (1.25 cm) thick rope and fasten ends to form a circle. Place on a greased baking sheet, cover and let rise in a warm place for 20 minutes. Bring 1 gallon (4.5 litres) of water to the boil in a large pot, lower the heat, and add 4 bagels. When bagels pop to the top of the water (about 2–3 minutes), remove to an ungreased baking sheet. Repeat method to cook the remaining bagels. Then bake in a preheated oven until browned. Allow bagels to cool before eating.
Variations: Sprinkle poppy seeds, sesame seeds, dried onion flakes, minced garlic or coarse salt over the tops of bagels while they are still wet from boiling.

Cholla – Berches

GERMANY   Stephanie Straus

Makes 2 small chollas   **Preparation 30 mins**   **Resting time 1½ hrs**
                                   Gas No 7, 425°F, 220°C   Cook 45 mins

17 oz potatoes prepared previous day (500 g)   ½ pt lukewarm water (¼ litre)
17 oz flour, sieved (500 g)   1 tsp sugar
1 dsp dried active yeast   2 tsp salt

The day before you want to bake, boil the potatoes in their skins and when cold peel
and grate them and spread them out to dry on a large plate. Old potatoes are best as
they do not have so much moisture.
Very important: When baking with yeast, everything has to be warm.
Take some of the lukewarm water, stir in sugar and scatter in the yeast – it will dissolve.
Make a dent in the centre of the flour and pour in the made up yeast. Put the two
teaspoons of salt around the rim of the bowl (because salt kills the yeast) and put in a
warm place.
When the yeast has started to make bubbles, add the potatoes and remaining
lukewarm water and begin kneading. Transfer to a floured board and knead for 10
minutes. The dough must be very firm. If it is not, add some more flour. Put the ball of
dough into a clean, floured bowl, cover and set to rise in a warm place until it has at
least doubled its size.
Put dough back onto floured board, knead well, then divide into 4 – two pieces for the
bases and the other two each divided into three, plaited and placed lightly on top of
bases. Brush the chollas with egg or salt water and sprinkle with poppyseeds. Cover
with oiled clingfilm and set to rise until nice and high. Bake in preheated oven for 10
minutes on Gas No 7, 425°F, 220°C, then for 30–35 minutes on Gas 6, 400°F, 200°C.

Fruit Loaves for Chanukah

SWITZERLAND   Lys Kenley

Preparation 25 mins   **Gas No 5, 375°F, 190°C**   **Cook 1–1½ hrs**   **Advance**

2½ lb dried pears (1.5 kg)   3½ oz orange peel (100 g)
17 oz dried figs (500 g)   7 oz hazelnuts (200 g)
3½ oz candied lemon peel (100 g)   9 oz sultanas (250 g)
7 oz almonds (200 g)   1 tsp cinnamon
9 oz walnuts (250 g)   1½ lb dark bread dough from a bakery
2–3 tbls kirsch   (750 g)
1½ lb dried prunes, stoned (750 g)

Soak pears, cook and drain. Chop all the nuts and fruit. Mix well with all other
ingredients, form into individual loaves and bake for a minimum of 1 hour (depending
on tin sizes) in a preheated oven.

Biscuits

Chocolate Stanger – Biscuits

GERMANY

Avril Kleeman

Preparation 20 mins

Resting time overnight

8 oz chocolate, grated (225 g)
8 oz ground almonds, unpeeled (225 g)
4 oz caster sugar (115 g)

1 small egg
Vanilla essence
Juice of 1 lemon

Mix chocolate and almonds and add all the other ingredients. Put in fridge to rest for about an hour, then roll out into a long sausage shape and cut into biscuits. Sprinkle a wooden board or baking tray with icing sugar, place biscuits on the tray. Flatten the tops with a knife. Leave in a cool room to dry out overnight. Turn biscuits over once. No cooking is needed. When dry and hard, ice with a lemon-flavoured icing.

Little Dutch Hamans

HOLLAND

Adele Schaverien

Preparation 20 mins   **Resting time 30 mins**   **Gas No 4, 350°F, 185°C**
Cook 12–20 mins

3 lb plain flour, sifted (1.4 kg)
½ cup cold water
1 tsp salt
1 tsp cinnamon
1 tsp ground cloves
2 oz shortening (55 g)
8 oz soft brown sugar (225 g)
8 oz molasses (225 g)
1 tsp allspice
1 tsp ginger
2 tsp bicarbonate of soda

Frosting
1 cup icing sugar
2 tbls water
½ tsp vanilla essence

To decorate
Currants
Slivered almonds
Cinnamon
Chocolate drops

Mix together the fat, sugar, molasses and water, stirring well until blended. Sift the flour and spices and remaining dry ingredients into a bowl and add the sugar/fat mixture. Work all ingredients together (by hand or machine) until they form a dough. Wrap in greaseproof paper or clingfilm and refrigerate for 30 minutes.
Split the dough into manageable pieces and roll out to a ½" (1.25 cm) thickness on a floured board. Using a gingerbread cutter, cut dough into shapes and place on a well-greased baking tray. Bake for 12–20 minutes. When cool spread with frosting (made by mixing all ingredients together) and decorate.

A Purim recipe.

Kichels

POLAND   Renee Linder

Preparation 10 mins   Refrigerate 20 mins   Gas No 6, 400°F, 200°C   Cook 25 mins

1 lb S.R. flour (450 g)
4 oz Tomor margarine (115 g)
4 oz white fat or butter (115 g)
2 eggs (size 1)

1 egg, beaten
6 oz caster sugar (170 g)
Sugar and cinnamon to sprinkle

Sieve the flour. Grate fat into flour and then add sugar and rub in. Add 2 eggs and mix into a dough. Refrigerate for 20 minutes. Roll out (not too thinly) and cut into round shapes or as desired. Brush with beaten egg and sprinkle with sugar and cinnamon mixture. Bake in oven for 15 minutes on the middle shelf. Then transfer to a higher shelf until golden brown.

Kussen – Passover Biscuits

ENGLAND   Laurie Samuels

Preparation 15 mins   Gas No 3, 325°F, 180°C   Cook 30 mins approx   Advance

2 egg whites
4 oz walnuts (115 g)
4 oz stoneless dates (115 g)

4 oz icing sugar, sifted (115 g)
4 oz blanched almonds (115 g)

Roughly chop the nuts and dates. Beat the egg whites until they stand in stiff, glossy peaks. Then add the icing sugar, a dessertspoonful at a time, beating after each addition until a stiff meringue is formed. Fold in the nuts and dates. Drop in small heaps on oiled baking trays. Bake until crisp and golden.

Lebkuchen – Biscuits

GERMANY   Avril Kleeman

Preparation 10 mins   Refrigerate 30 mins   Gas No 4, 350°F, 185°C   Cook 25 mins

2 eggs
6 oz sugar (170 g)
1 oz candied peel (25 g)
8 oz almonds (225 g)
½ tsp ground cloves

1 tsp cinnamon
1 tsp mixed spice
1 dsp flour
⅓ tsp baking powder
Rice paper

Beat the sugar and eggs. Mix in all remaining ingredients, the baking powder last of all. Put mixture in fridge for 30 minutes. Form into small round balls, place them on rice paper on a greased baking sheet and bake.

Nut Slices

ENGLAND   Ruth Cohen

Preparation 15 mins Gas No 3, 325°F, 180°C Cook 35–40 mins Advance Freezable

Topping
1½ oz flour (40 g)
1 cup sugar
¾ cup desiccated coconut
3 eggs, lightly beaten
¾ cup chopped walnuts
1 tbls ground almonds
¾ cup glacé cherries, coarsely cut
Few drops almond essence

Base
4 oz flour (115 g)
2 oz sugar (55 g)
2 oz butter (55 g)

12″ × 9″ greased baking tray (32 × 25 cm)

Base: Mix flour and sugar and then rub in butter to form crumbs. Press these into baking tray.
Topping: Mix all ingredients together and spread over the crumb base. Bake until golden brown and firm to the touch. Cut into small squares and leave in tin until cold. Store in airtight box or freeze to maintain freshness.

Pentecost Biscuits

ENGLAND

Preparation 15 mins   Gas No 4, 350°F, 185°C   Cook 15 mins   Advance

8 oz flour (225 g)
4 oz caster sugar (115 g)
4 oz butter (115 g)

1 egg
1 tsp noyau (almond liqueur)
Citron peel

Reserve part of the white of the egg and 1 oz (25 g) of the sugar for decoration. Place the butter in a basin and stand it on top of the oven for 2–3 minutes to soften (but not to the consistency of oil). Mix in the flour and sugar and add the beaten egg and noyau. Make into a stiff paste. Turn onto a floured board, roll out thinly and cut into shapes with small round cutters or with the top of a wineglass. Place biscuits on a floured baking tin, brush with the reserved white of egg and sprinkle with caster sugar. Place a piece of citron peel in the centre of each biscuit. Bake, then put on a wire tray to cool.

Served at Shavuot.

Sakostina Coulouraiga – Biscuits

GREECE

Preparation 15 mins   Gas No 4, 350°F, 185°C   Cook 10 mins approx   Advance

7 glasses flour
1½ glasses sugar
1 small coffee cup cognac
Gin, sufficient to mix to dough
Sesame seeds

1 glass sunflower oil
1 glass orange juice
5 tsp baking powder
1 level tsp cinnamon

Mix flour, sugar and oil together. Add other ingredients, then enough gin to make a light dough. Shape the biscuits (usually finger shapes), dip in sesame seeds and bake until lightly browned.

Boterkoek – Shortbread

HOLLAND   Nanny ten Brink-de Lieme

Preparation 10 mins   Gas No 7, 425°F, 220°C   Cook 35 mins approx   Advance

11 oz flour (315 g)
8 oz granulated sugar (225 g)
8 oz unsalted butter (225 g)

Pinch of salt
Beaten egg to glaze (optional)

Mix all the ingredients together by hand. Put the dough in a greased shallow baking tin. Brush top with cold water or egg to glaze and prick with a fork. Bake until light brown on the outside and soft on the inside.

Dutch Butter Cake – Shortbread

HOLLAND   Rae Neiman

Preparation 15 mins   Gas No 5, 375°F, 190°C   Cook 30 mins

8 oz plain flour (225 g)
6 oz caster sugar (170 g)
½ tsp almond or vanilla essence
6 oz butter (170 g)
1 egg, separated

To decorate
Blanched almonds

7" baking tin (18 cm)

Sieve the flour and sugar into a large bowl, rub in the butter until a breadcrumb texture. Then add the egg yolk and essence (you can use a food processor for this operation, but take care not to overbeat once the egg is in). If you are mixing by hand, knead lightly until it is a soft ball, pat gently into well-greased baking tin and brush the top with the lightly beaten egg white, taking care to leave a space around the edge. Sprinkle with a few blanched almonds and bake for about 30 minutes. After removing from oven, leave for a moment then cut into squares or preferred shapes. Remove from tin when cool. Delicious on day of baking.

Preissel Kuchen – Quick Shortbread

GERMANY   Mrs H.E. Kochmann

Preparation 5 mins   **Gas No 4, 350°F, 185°C**   **Cook 20–25 mins**   **Advance**

13½ oz plain flour (375 g)
8½ oz butter (250 g)
4½ oz caster sugar (125 g)
1 packet vanilla sugar (15 g)

To decorate
Caster sugar

13½" × 10½" (33 × 25 cm) baking tin

Mix ingredients until crumbly and spread evenly on the greased baking tin. Bake until golden brown, when the base will have formed and the top will still be crumbly. Cut into fingers or other shapes immediately after removing from oven and sprinkle with caster sugar. Remove from tin when cool.

Vanilla Kipferl

AUSTRIA

Preparation 20 mins   **Gas No 4, 350°F, 185°C**   **Cook 20–30 mins**   **Advance**

5 oz plain flour (145 g)
4 oz unsalted butter (115 g), cut into pieces
2 oz ground almonds (55 g)

2 oz caster sugar (55 g)
2 packets vanilla sugar (30 g)
Icing sugar for coating

Mix all ingredients on a board using only one packet of vanilla sugar. Form into moon shapes and bake on a tray lined with Bakewell paper. While shapes are still warm roll them in icing sugar mixed with the second packet of vanilla sugar.

CAKES

Small Cakes

Blueberry Muffins

CANADA   Betty Crystal

Preparation 10 mins   Gas No 5, 375°F, 190°C   **Cook 15–20 mins approx**

¼ cup soft butter   ½ tsp salt
¾ cup sugar   2 tsp baking powder
1 egg, well beaten   ½ cup milk
1½ cups flour   1 cup blueberries, fresh or frozen

In a bowl, cream together the butter and sugar, add the egg and mix well. Add sifted dry ingredients alternately with the milk. Fold in the blueberries and pour mixture into buttered muffin tins, filling each ⅔ full. Bake.

Bublanina – Fruit Sponge Cake

CZECHOSLOVAKIA   Nini Orsten

Preparation 15 mins   Gas No 4, 350°F, 185°C   **Cook 45 mins**

2 large eggs, weighed   *Topping*
S.R. flour, same weight as eggs   Cherries, apricots or plums, sliced
A little grated lemon rind
Sugar, same weight as eggs   10½" × 7" × 2" baking tin (27 × 18 × 4 cm)
Butter, half weight of eggs

Beat egg yolks with sugar and butter until creamy. Whisk egg whites in a separate bowl and then fold whites and flour into yolk mixture. Pour into greased and floured baking tin. On top of the mixture arrange cherries, apricots or plums in rows. Bake until light brown. To serve, cut into squares.

Caruso

CZECHOSLOVAKIA   Hana Samson

Preparation 10 mins   **Gas No 4, 350°F, 185°C**   **Cook 20 mins approx**

5 oz butter (140 g)
4 eggs, separated
4 oz finely ground almonds (115 g)
4 oz caster sugar (115 g)

3½ oz dark plain chocolate, melted (100 g)
To serve
Vanilla flavoured whipped cream and icing
   sugar

Line a Swiss roll tin with greaseproof paper which has been greased and sprinkled with flour or matzo meal. Cream butter and sugar and then add egg yolks. Mix thoroughly. In a separate bowl whisk egg whites until very stiff. To butter mixture add cooled melted chocolate and ground almonds and then, with a large metal spoon, carefully fold in egg whites. Bake in a moderate oven until the top is springy. When cold, cut in half and sandwich with vanilla flavoured whipped cream. Sprinkle top with icing sugar and cut into squares with a very sharp knife.

Kousmeri – Cheese Cake

GREECE

Preparation 15 mins   **Gas No 4, 350°F, 185°C**   **Cook 30 mins approx**

2 lb soft white unsalted cheese or feta
   (900 g)
4 eggs
¾ cup sugar
1½ cups flour
6 tbls melted butter

Syrup
1 cup water
¼ cup honey
½ cup sugar
Juice of 1 lemon (optional)

9″ × 12″ baking tin (22 × 30 cm)

Syrup: Boil all ingredients together until they form a syrup thick enough to coat the back of a spoon. Chill.
Cake: Mash the cheese in a large bowl until creamy (a little yoghurt can be added if it is too thick). Add the eggs, sugar and flour and beat well. Stir in the melted butter and pour the mixture into well-greased baking tin. Bake until golden. Remove from oven, and while still hot, pour over the well-chilled syrup. Serve cold, cut into squares.

Traditionally served at Shavuot.

Ciambelle – Doughnuts

ITALY

Makes 25

Preparation 40 mins

Cook 15 mins

12 oz flour (350 g)
3½ oz caster sugar (100 g)
1 oz fresh yeast (30 g)
½ cup olive oil
½ tsp vanilla essence
½ tsp cinnamon

2 eggs, beaten
Grated rind of ½ lemon
Oil for frying
Decoration
Caster sugar

Place the yeast with half the flour and half a cup of lukewarm water in a large bowl, mix and cover bowl with a cloth. Leave in a warm place until the mixture becomes frothy. Add another half a cup of lukewarm water, the eggs, sugar, oil, vanilla, cinnamon, lemon rind and flour. Knead until the dough is soft and elastic.
Sprinkle flour onto a wooden board. Place the dough on it. Pat it with your hands until it is 1" (3 cm) thick, then cut out the doughnuts with a large round cutter and make small holes in the middle with a smaller cutter. Fry the doughnuts, in deep fat, a few at a time, until they are golden brown on one side, then turn them over and fry the other side. Remove from oil, drain the doughnuts well and sprinkle with sugar. Serve hot.

Traditionally served with coffee to break the Yom Kippur fast.

Danish Pastries

ENGLAND

Ruth Shire

Preparation 25 mins

Resting time 2 hrs approx

Gas No 4, 350°F, 185°C
Cook 30 mins

Dough
8 oz flour (225 g)
1 packet dried yeast
½ cup warmed milk
1 egg, lightly beaten

Filling
6 oz margarine (170 g)
2–3 oz plain flour (55–85 g)
Marzipan
Icing
Icing sugar
Rum

Mix yeast with the lukewarm milk, flour and egg. Cover with greased clingfilm or a towel and leave in a warm place for approximately 40 minutes until it has nearly doubled in volume. Meanwhile, make the filling by rubbing the margarine into the flour to make breadcrumbs.
Roll out the dough thinly into a rectangular shape, sprinkle the filling on top and fold over into three. Place in fridge for 15 minutes. Roll out again into a large rectangle, fold into three again and put back into fridge. Repeat this process four more times.
Roll the pastry for the final time into ¼" (⅔ cm) thickness. Cut into triangles and fill with the marzipan. Roll into crescents and bake.
When cooked and slightly cooled, ice with rum-flavoured icing.

Kiesjelish

HOLLAND   Nielske Spiero

Preparation 10 mins   **Resting time 1 hr**   **Cook 5 mins**

17 oz flour (500 g)   4 eggs
4 tbls cold water   Pinch of salt
Sunflower oil for frying   Icing sugar for dusting

Sift the flour into a bowl and add the eggs, water and salt and knead thoroughly. Roll the dough in clingfilm and put it in the refrigerator for 1 hour. Roll dough very thinly and cut into 2½" (7 cm) squares. Heat the oil and fry the dough squares a couple at a time until brown. Drain and then sprinkle with icing sugar.

These are served at Purim.

Linzerschnitten

AUSTRIA

Makes 1 tray   **Preparation 15 mins**   **Gas No 4, 350°F, 185°C**   **Cook 30 mins**

5 oz caster sugar (145 g)   5 oz flour (145 g)
5 oz unsalted butter (145 g), cut into pieces   2 egg yolks
5 oz ground walnuts (145 g)   ½ tsp mixed spice
½ lb morello cherry jam (225 g)   ½ tsp cinnamon

Mix all ingredients except jam on a board. Spread half the mixture on a floured tray, spread jam on top. Roll the remainder of the mixture between your hands into strips and make a lattice pattern over the jam. Bake. Cut into squares while still hot, remove and cool on a baking rack. Makes 1 tray.

Nuss-schnitten

CZECHOSLOVAKIA   Ruth Arnold

Preparation 15 mins   **Gas No 3, 325°F, 180°C**   **Cook 30 mins approx**   **Advance**

5 oz sugar (140 g)   ½ oz medium matzo meal (15 g)
4 eggs, separated   5 oz grated nuts (140 g)
6 oz chocolate, grated (170 g)   *Glaze*
                                             Orange or lemon icing

Beat yolks with sugar until white. Fold in grated chocolate, nuts and matzo meal. Beat egg whites stiffly and then fold into chocolate mixture and spoon into a Swiss roll tin. Bake. When cooked cut into slices and glaze with orange or lemon icing.

Orgeadebolus

HOLLAND   Lizzy Kukenheim

Preparation 30 mins   Standing time 1 hr   Gas No 6, 400°F, 200°C   Cook 50 mins

Dough
11½ oz flour (325 g)
1 egg
2 oz sugar (50 g)
½ oz yeast (15 g)
2 cups of lukewarm milk
3½ oz butter (100 g)
2½ oz icing sugar (75 g)

Filling
5½ oz ground almonds (150 g)
1 tsp sugar
Grated rind of 1 orange
1–2 tbls melted butter
Syrup
3 oz sugar (80 g)
15 fl oz water (½ litre)
4 oz butter (115 g)
1 packet vanilla sugar (15 g)

Dough: Dissolve the yeast in the milk. Beat the egg with the sugar, then add egg mixture, yeast mixture and butter to the flour in a large warmed bowl. Knead until the dough is elastic, then let it rise, in a warm place, covered lightly with a cloth, for approximately 40 minutes. Divide the dough into 8 pieces and roll each into a rectangle approximately 2″ × 5″ (5 × 12 cm). Cover the rectangles with icing sugar.
Filling: Mix together ground almonds, sugar, orange rind and melted butter. Spread mixture over dough rectangles, roll up and coil each one into a snail-shell shape. Leave to rise for 15 minutes in a warm place.
Syrup: Dissolve sugar in the water. Add butter and vanilla sugar, and cook until thickened.
Bake the shapes. During baking, cover the shapes with the syrup several times. When cooked, remove from the oven and cover shapes with the remaining syrup. Eat while warm.
Alternative Filling and Syrup
Filling: 10½ oz stem ginger, chopped (300 g); 1 cup ginger juice; 1 oz butter (25 g); fine breadcrumbs.
Syrup: 1 cup water; 1 cup ginger juice; 2 oz butter (50 g); 1 oz sugar (25 g).

Large Cakes

Almond Cake

GERMANY   Lottie Freedman

Preparation 15 mins   **Gas No 4, 350°F, 185°C**   **Cook 40 mins**   **Advance**

8 eggs, separated
8 oz sugar (225 g)
1 small glass of rum

8 oz ground almonds (225 g)
1 tsp vanilla essence
1 dsp cake matzo meal

10″ loose-bottomed cake tin (26 cm)

Mix sugar and egg yolks and beat slowly until mixture is white and beaters leave a trail. Add ground almonds, vanilla essence, rum and cake matzo meal and mix well. Whisk egg whites in a separate bowl until stiff and then fold into yolk mixture. Pour into greased tin and bake.

Traditionally served at Pesach.

Apple Cake I

GERMANY   Mrs E. Faerber

Preparation 20 mins   **Resting time 20 mins**   **Gas No 4, 350°F, 185°C**   **Cook 1 hr**
                                                                        Advance

10 oz S.R. flour (285 g)
3 oz caster sugar (85 g)
1½ lb cooking apples, peeled and sliced
    (675 g)
5 oz butter or margarine (145 g)
Pinch of cinnamon

1 oz currants (25 g)
1 oz sultanas (25 g)
1 oz candied peel (25 g)
Brown sugar

8″ loose-bottomed tart tin (20 cm)

Grease the tart tin. Stew apples in very little water with currants and sultanas. Cook to a pulp, then sweeten to taste with brown sugar and add chopped peel. Leave until cold.
Rub butter into flour, add caster sugar and egg and knead to a pliable dough. Leave to rest for 20 minutes, then roll out into a long strip, fold in three and then roll again. Repeat this process once more. Line bottom and sides of tin with pastry. Sprinkle with extra caster sugar and flour. Pour in apple and decorate with strips of pastry. Bake tart, covered with an enamel plate, for ¾ hour. Remove plate and continue cooking for another 15 minutes. Leave in tin until cold.

Apple Cake II

POLAND   Valerie Greenbury

Preparation 25 mins   Resting time 30 mins   Gas No 4, 350°F, 185°C   Cook 55 mins
Advance   Freezable

Pastry
1 lb S.R. flour (450 g)
8 oz hard margarine (225 g)
2 dsp caster sugar
A few drops almond essence
1 egg, beaten together with a little milk or water

Filling
Red jam
Handful chopped nuts
Handful dried fruit
1 tsp cinnamon
Sugar
A little lemon juice
3 large cooking apples, finely sliced
To decorate
1 tsp caster sugar

Line a Swiss roll tin with foil and grease. Do not bend the edges of foil over the side until after the top layer of pastry goes on.

Mix flour, margarine and sugar into breadcrumbs and add liquid ingredients. Knead into pastry dough. Refrigerate for about 30 minutes. Cut into two pieces, allowing a little less pastry for the base. Roll out (not too thinly) to line the tin and prick the dough. Put a thin layer of jam on the pastry and cover with sliced apples. Sprinkle sugar, spices, lemon juice, nuts and dried fruit over apples. Roll out the top layer of pastry, damp the edges with water. Cover tin and press edges of pastry together. Brush the top with milk and sprinkle with sugar, cinnamon and a few chopped nuts. Before cooking make square indentations across and down so that it will be easier to cut into pieces. If the pastry is browning too quickly while cooking, lay a sheet of greaseproof paper on the top towards the end of the baking time. When cool, unravel foil edges and lift apple cake from tin.

Austrian Gateau

AUSTRIA   Joan Rosenberg

Preparation 15 mins Gas No 5, 375°F, 190°C Cook 10–15 mins Advance Freezable

Gateau
6 eggs
5 oz ground almonds (145 g)
3 oz grated chocolate or vermicelli (85 g)
4½ oz caster sugar (125 g)
1 tsp almond essence

Topping
4 oz margarine (115 g)
1 egg
1 packet vanilla sugar (15 g)
4 oz caster sugar (115 g)
3 oz melted chocolate (85 g)

1 large Swiss roll tin, lined with silicone
   paper

Gateau: Separate eggs and beat whites until peaked. Add 1½ oz sugar (40 g) and beat. Beat egg yolks with remaining sugar until it is like a cream. Add ground almonds, essence and grated chocolate. Fold whites into mixture and put into Swiss roll tin. Bake for 10 minutes or until cooked. When cool, remove silicone paper and cut into 4 equal pieces.
Topping: Cream margarine and sugar together and then beat in egg, melted chocolate and vanilla sugar. Sandwich mixture between quarters and over the top and sides of gateau.

Milchike Babke

SOUTH AFRICA   Rebecca Symons

Preparation 20 mins   **Rising time 1 hr**   **Gas No 6, 400°F, 200°C**
                                                          Cook 30 mins approx

2 lb white flour (900 g)
2 oz cake yeast (50 g)
8 oz butter (225 g)
1¼ cups sugar
1 tsp salt

1 cup lukewarm water
3 size 2 eggs, beaten
1 cup milk
Filling
Raisins, sultanas, sugar and cinnamon

Mix yeast with the water. Leave in a warm place and allow to become frothy. Make a well in the flour, mix in the yeast with a fork and allow to rise. Melt butter in the milk and add with other ingredients to the risen dough. Beat well with a spoon until mixture is smooth, allow to rise. Knead well and allow to rise again. Either shape into buns, filling with raisins, sultanas, sugar and cinnamon or make into loaves by rolling out into rectangles and sprinkling with cinnamon and sugar, or cinnamon, sugar, raisins and sultanas. Bake.

Brauner Kirschenkuchen

CZECHOSLOVAKIA   Ruth Arnold

Preparation 20 mins   **Gas No 4, 350°F, 185°C**   **Cook ¾–1 hr**   **Advance**

3½ oz margarine (100 g)   ½ tsp baking powder
3 egg whites, beaten   1½ oz chocolate, melted (45 g)
3 egg yolks and 1 whole egg   1 tbls rum
5 oz sugar (140 g)   40 cherries (drain if tinned)
3 oz breadcrumbs/matzo meal (85 g)
2 oz ground almonds (55 g)   10" spring-form cake tin (25 cm)

Mix together breadcrumbs, ground almonds and baking powder. Beat margarine with the sugar until well creamed. Then add egg yolks and whole egg and beat thoroughly. Add dry ingredients gently and then fold in egg whites that have already been beaten until in peaks. Spoon into cake tin, place cherries on top and bake.

Cheese Cake

AUSTRIA

Preparation 20 mins   **Gas No 4, 350°F, 185°C**   **Cook 1 hr**   **Advance**

10 sponge fingers, crumbled   11 dsp caster sugar
4 oz unsalted butter (115 g)   2 lb curd cheese (900 g)
3 eggs, separated   1 packet vanilla sugar (15 g)
1 dsp S.R. flour
                                           12" baking tin (30 cm)

Butter baking tin and place some of the crumbled sponge fingers on the base and sides. Beat egg whites and reserve. Beat butter in mixer until almost white and add all other ingredients, including the 3 egg yolks. Mix well. Fold in egg whites. Put mixture into tin and place remainder of crumbled sponge fingers on the top. Bake for 1 hour, then turn off oven and leave cake inside for 20 minutes to cool. Serve warm.

Grandma Sally's Cheesecake

ENGLAND   Sally Bloom

Preparation 15 mins   **Pastry resting time 30 mins**   **Gas No 4, 350°F, 185°C**
                                                                         Cook 40 mins approx

Pastry
8 oz S.R. flour (225 g) *or* 1 tbls less + 1 tbls
    custard powder
4 oz butter (115 g)
3 oz sugar (85 g)
1 large egg, beaten

Filling
1 lb cooking cheese (450 g)
2 small eggs
2 fl oz double cream (55 ml)
3½ tbls sugar
2 oz butter (55 g)
Sultanas (optional)

8″ flan dish (20 cm)

Pastry: Place flour in bowl, add butter cut into small pieces and mix until resembling fine breadcrumbs. Add sugar. Mix in the egg until it becomes a ball. Wrap in greaseproof paper and refrigerate for 30 minutes. Roll out, line flan dish and bake blind until golden brown (approximately 15 mins).
Filling: Beat cheese slowly. Add softened butter and beat again. Add sugar and eggs and beat. Mix in cream. Pour into prepared flan case. Decorate with strips of pastry if desired. Bake for 25 minutes or until cheese has *just* set.

Cheese Cake

RUSSIA   Mila Griesel

Preparation 10 mins   **Gas No 4, 350°F, 185°C**   **Cook 1½ hrs**   **Refrigerate 1 day**
                                                                              Advance

4 trifle sponges or stale cake
1 lb curd cheese (450 g)
4 oz sugar (115 g)
4 eggs, separated
4 oz butter (115 g)

4 drops lemon juice
Handful cornflour
5 fl oz double cream (140 ml)
Optional
Raisins, dried fruit, chocolate vermicelli,
    whipped cream

Line a cake tin with greased greaseproof paper and spread with crumbled sponges or cake. Beat egg whites until fluffy. Mix rest of cake ingredients, then fold in egg whites and spread mixture over base. Cook until set and light brown. Refrigerate for 1 day. The cake will drop a little, but you can cover with whipped cream/fruit/chocolate if desired.

Cherry Cake

HUNGARY   Vera Grodzinski

Preparation 10 mins   **Gas No 5, 375°F, 190°C**   **Cook 30 mins approx**   **Advance**

4 oz sugar (115 g)
3 eggs
5 oz S.R. flour (145 g)
2 lb sour/sweet cherries (900 g) or 2 lb jar
 Hungarian/Polish sour cherries (900 g)

Pinch of salt
Little grated lemon rind (optional)
1 glass milk

8″ cake tin, greased (20 cm)

If using fresh cherries stew lightly and then allow to cool. Beat sugar and eggs until well mixed. Add flour and lemon rind, then the glass of milk. Pour mixture into cake tin. Drain cherries and add to cake mixture. Bake until cake mixture is cooked.

My grandmother would always have these ingredients at home as it is a quick recipe which can be served hot or cold to unexpected guests. Can be served with tea or coffee or as a dessert, on its own or with ice cream.

Chocolate and Almond Cake

GERMANY   Herta Linden

Preparation 10 mins   **Gas No 4, 350°F, 185°C**   **Cook 30 mins**

8 oz butter or margarine (225 g)
8 oz ground almonds (225 g)
3½ oz S.R. flour (100 g)

8 oz sugar (225 g)
4 eggs, separated
½ oz cocoa (15 g)

Grease a large flan tin or two sandwich tins. Cream butter and sugar. Add egg yolks and beat well. Add flour and almonds. Lastly fold in well-beaten egg whites, pour into tin and bake in a moderate oven. If making two cakes, sandwich them together with whipped cream or chocolate icing.

Chocolate Half-and-Half Cake

ROMANIA   Hermy Jankel

Preparation 20 mins   **Gas No 5, 375°F, 190°C**   **Cook 1 hr**   **Advance**

Cake
8 oz unsalted butter, softened (225 g)
6 eggs, separated
8 oz cooking chocolate (225 g)
4 heaped tbls breadcrumbs or cake matzo
   meal
8 oz caster sugar (225 g)

Topping
2 tbls sugar
2 tbls water
4 oz whole almonds, with skins

9″ or 10″ loose-bottomed or spring-form tin
   (22 or 25 cm)

Cake: Melt chocolate in a double saucepan or microwave. Beat egg yolks and caster sugar then beat in butter and melted chocolate. Fold in stiffly beaten egg whites and divide mixture between two bowls. Add breadcrumbs or cake meal to one half of mixture, spoon into greased cake tin and bake for 40 minutes in moderate oven Gas 5, 375°F, 190°C, then turn down to Gas No 2, 300°F, 150°C for 10 minutes. Turn off oven, open oven door and leave cake to cool. Pour remaining mixture over cake, leaving cooked cake in tin.
Topping: Using a strong saucepan, caramelise all ingredients until light brown. Pour onto a wet board and leave until cold. Break up with rolling pin and sprinkle over cake.

Chocolate Loaf

GERMANY   Lottie Freedman

Preparation 15 mins   **Gas No 4, 350°F, 185°C**   **Cook 45 mins**   **Advance**

Cake
8 oz margarine (225 g)
4 oz icing sugar (115 g)
4 eggs, separated
4 oz melted chocolate (115 g)
4 oz unpeeled almonds, ground (115 g)
1 dsp medium matzo meal

Icing
3 oz melted chocolate (85 g)
3 oz icing sugar (85 g)
1 dsp water
1 dsp cocoa
2 oz butter (55 g)

To decorate
Split almonds

Mix margarine and icing sugar until creamy, add egg yolks and melted chocolate with the rest of the ingredients. Fold in the beaten egg whites. Bake in a greased loaf tin. Mix icing ingredients together in a saucepan and heat until chocolate and butter have melted, taking care not to let it boil. When cake has cooled, ice it and decorate with almonds.

Tante Hedda's Schokolade Kuchen

AUSTRIA   Suzy Landes

Serves 10–12   **Preparation 10 mins**   **Gas No 6, 400°F, 200°C**   **Cook 40 mins**

Cake
8 oz caster sugar (225 g)
8 oz butter (225 g)
7 eggs, separated
5 oz flour (145 g)
8 oz chocolate, melted (225 g)
Handful of ground hazelnuts/walnuts
   (optional)

Glaze
4 fl oz double cream (115 ml)
1 oz butter (25 g)
4 oz cooking chocolate (115 g)

10″ spring-form cake tin, greased (25 cm)

Blend sugar and butter. When light and fluffy, add egg yolks, melted chocolate and nuts if desired. Fold in flour. Whisk egg whites in a separate bowl and then fold into mixture. Bake in a greased cake tin.
Glaze: Heat cream and then add butter and chocolate. When blended pour over cake and allow to cool.

Alsace Cinnamon Cake

FRANCE   Odette Dreyfuss

Preparation 15 mins   **Resting time 30 mins**   **Gas No 3, 325°F, 180°C**
                                                                     Cook 40 mins approx

Cake
5 egg yolks
8¾ oz unsalted butter (250 g)
8¾ oz caster sugar (250 g)
14 oz plain flour (400 g)
Pinch of salt
1 full glass of kirsch

Topping
1 egg yolk
Cinnamon
Sugar

½″ deep baking tray (1½ cm)

Cream butter, egg yolks and sugar, add kirsch and salt. Add flour and make into a dough. Knead the dough, then leave to rest for a while. Grease baking tray, place dough in tin and smooth the top. With a pastry wheel mark out into squares. Brush the top of the cake with the egg yolk and sprinkle with sugar and cinnamon mixture. Bake.

Equal Weight Cake

CZECHOSLOVAKIA   Helen Reisman

Preparation 20 mins   Gas No 4, 350°F, 185°C   Cook 30 mins approx

4 eggs (weighed in shells)
Caster sugar, butter and flour in equal
   weight to eggs (remove 4 tbls flour and
   discard)
4 tbls ground almonds

Decoration
Pitted cherries, sliced apricots, plums or
   peaches (not berries)
Icing sugar

Separate yolks and whites of eggs. Beat egg whites stiffly and reserve. In another bowl, cream butter and sugar and then add flour and almonds, mixing gently. Fold in egg whites. Spread on a greased Swiss roll tin lined with baking paper. Bake. When cool, decorate with fruit and sprinkle with icing sugar.

Fluden

HUNGARY   Ilona Grunberger

Preparation 25 mins   Resting time 30 mins   Gas No 6, 400°F, 200°C   Cook 40 mins
Advance

Dough
18 oz plain flour (500 g)
11 oz butter/margarine (300 g)
4 eggs
3½ oz sugar (100 g)
½ oz fresh yeast (15 g)
8 tbls kosher sweet wine

Filling
9 oz walnuts (250 g)
Handful of raisins
4 tbls honey
2 apples, grated
Cinnamon and sugar to taste
Prune jam
1 egg beaten

Dough: Dissolve the yeast in a small amount of water. Blend together the flour, sugar, fat, eggs and wine and work the yeast into the flour mixture. Let the dough rest in a warm place and when risen, divide equally into four pieces.
Roll out each piece into a thin rectangular sheet. Generously spread one sheet with prune jam and cover with another sheet of dough; spread this with grated apple and sprinkle with sugar and cinnamon. Cover this filling with the third sheet, and spread with a mixture of honey, walnuts and raisins. Cover with the last sheet of dough and brush with beaten egg. Bake until golden.

Served at Purim.

Fruit Bread

GERMANY   Mrs Kochmann

Preparation 10 mins   Gas No 4, 350°F, 185°C   Cook 45 mins approx   Advance

4½ oz caster sugar (125 g)
4½ oz split almonds (125 g)
8 oz raisins (225 g)
2½ oz currants (70 g)
7 oz sultanas (200 g)
4½ oz S.R. flour, sieved (125 g)

Pinch baking powder
3 eggs
½ tsp cinnamon

2 lb loaf tin (900 g)

Beat eggs and sugar until creamy. Add nuts, fruit and cinnamon. Fold in the flour and baking powder. Place in a greased and lined loaf tin and bake until just firm.

Griestorte

CZECHOSLOVAKIA   Mariette Demuth

Preparation 10 mins   Gas No 4, 350°F, 185°C   Cook approx 45 mins   Advance

8 oz caster sugar (225 g)
1 lemon, rind and juice
4 oz semolina (115 g)
6 egg yolks

20 almonds, ground with skins
6 egg whites, whisked until stiff
Garnish
Whipped cream and fruit

Mix sugar and yolks thoroughly, then add lemon juice and rind, ground almonds and semolina. Fold in egg whites. Pour mixture into greased cake tin and bake. Serve cooled cake with whipped cream, raspberries, strawberries or any other fruit.

Gugelhopf – Without Yeast

AUSTRIA   Herta Pilchik

Preparation 20 mins   Gas No 6, 400°F, 200°C   Cook 1 hr approx

5½ oz butter (150 g)
5½ oz sugar (150 g)
9 tbls milk
Pinch of salt
Icing sugar

3 eggs, separated
2 tbls rum
10 oz S.R. flour (280 g)
Sultanas to taste

8″ cake tin (20 cm), buttered and floured

Cream butter and sugar together. Add egg yolks to the creamed mixture with the rum. Add the milk gradually with the flour and salt. Beat the egg whites and add to the mixture with sultanas. Bake. Allow to cool a little in tin and when cold dust with icing sugar.

Hazelnut Sponge

GERMANY   Margit Silber

Preparation 20 mins   Gas No 4–5, 350°–375°F, 185°–190°C   Cook 30 mins approx

5 eggs, separated
4 oz hazelnuts, roasted and ground (115 g)
Little lemon juice
4 oz caster sugar (115 g)

1 tbls S.R. flour
Whipped cream and jam

Two 7″ sandwich tins, lined and greased
    (17.5 cm)

Beat egg yolks and sugar until creamy. Add hazelnuts, lemon juice and flour. Beat well. Whisk egg whites until quite stiff and fold into yolk mixture. Divide into 2 tins and bake until springy. Sandwich with cream and black cherry jam.

Honey Cake

ENGLAND   Beverley Stopler

**Preparation 20 mins   Gas No 2, 300°F, 160°C   Cook 1½ hrs approx   Advance
                                                                                    Freezable**

1 lb tin of golden syrup (450 g)
Same tin filled with caster sugar, then warm
    water and then corn oil
1 lb S.R. flour (450 g)
3 eggs
1 tsp mixed spice

1 tsp cinnamon
1 tsp baking powder
1 tsp ginger
1 tsp bicarbonate of soda
7 tbls kiddush wine

Beat eggs. Warm golden syrup, water, sugar and oil together until smooth and then allow to cool. Add to eggs. Sift together flour, mixed spice, ginger, cinnamon and baking powder. Add wine and bicarbonate of soda to egg mixture and mix well. Finally add sifted dry ingredients. Bake until firm.

Traditionally served at Rosh Hashana.

Aunt Sarah's Honey Cake

POLAND   Pat Julius

Preparation 10 mins   Gas No 4, 350°F, 185°C   Cook 2 hrs   Advance   Freezable

1 lb plain flour (450 g)
8 oz honey (225 g)
8 oz sugar (225 g)
2 eggs
1 cup oil
¾ cup warm water

2 tsp mixed spice
1 tsp cinnamon
1 tsp ginger
1 tsp bicarbonate of soda
1 tsp baking powder

Beat eggs, mix in sugar and then the oil. Continue adding remaining ingredients leaving the flour until last. Finally fold in the flour. Pour mixture into baking tin and cook for approximately 2 hours until centre is cooked when tested with a baking needle.

This is traditionally served at Rosh Hashana.

Tante Hedda's Kugelhupf

AUSTRIA   Suzy Landes

**Serves 8–10   Preparation 10 mins   Gas No 3, 325°F, 180°C   Cook 45 mins   Advance
Freezable**

8 oz butter or margarine (225 g)
4 eggs, separated
9 oz S.R. flour (250 g)
8 oz sugar (225 g)
Juice and rind of 1 lemon

Handful of hazelnuts (optional)

9″ Kugelhupf tin, greased and floured
(22 cm)

Cream butter and sugar, add egg yolks and lemon. Whisk egg whites in a separate bowl. Fold egg whites and flour into mixture. Put a layer of hazelnuts in bottom of tin, if desired. Then add mixture and cook.

Linzertorte

GERMANY   Rosemary Fisch

Preparation 15 mins   **Gas No 6, 400°F, 200°C**   **Cook 1 hr approx**   **Advance**

1¼ cups S.R. flour	1 cup sugar
1 tbls cocoa	2 eggs
½ tsp cinnamon	1 tsp grated lemon rind
¼ tsp ground cloves	1 cup ground unblanched almonds
¼ tsp salt	Jam or preserves
1 cup butter	

Sieve the cocoa, cinnamon, cloves, salt and flour together, 3 times. Cream the butter, beat in the sugar until light and fluffy. Add eggs one at a time, beating each for 1 minute. Add lemon rind with the nuts and mix thoroughly. Fold in the flour. If the dough mixture is too soft, chill for 30 minutes. Roll out dough between sheets of waxed paper to ⅛" thick (3.15 mm).
Line bottom and sides of a shallow baking tin with the dough and cover generously with jam or preserves. Roll out remaining dough and cut into strips. Use to make a lattice pattern over the jam. Bake. Before serving, fill in the hollows with additional jam or preserves.

Marillen Kuchen – Apricot or Plum Cake

AUSTRIA   Herta Pilchik

Preparation 15 mins   **Gas No 4, 350°F, 185°C**   **Cook 30 mins**   **Advance**

2 oz butter (50 g)	Rind and juice of 1 lemon
2½ oz sugar (70 g)	5¼ oz S.R. flour (140 g)
2 eggs	
7 tbls milk	Two 7" × 11" × 1" tins, greased and lined
1 lb plums or apricots, halved (450 g)	with bakewell paper (17 × 27 × 2.5 cm)

Cream butter and sugar together. Beat eggs and add them to the creamed mixture, then add the flour, milk, lemon rind and juice and mix the batter well. Pour mixture into tins and place plums or apricots on top and bake. This could be baked in 1 large tin instead.

Mohn Cake – Poppyseed

HUNGARY   Aniko Grunsfeld

Preparation 15 mins   **Gas No 2, 300°F, 160°C**   **Cook 1 hr**   **Advance**

Cake   *Topping*
10 eggs, separated   Juice of 1 lemon
2 cups caster sugar   1 lb icing sugar (450 g)
1 cup oil
1 lb poppyseeds, ground (450 g)   13″ × 9″ cake tin, greased (32 × 22 cm)
Juice and rind of 1 lemon
2 tbls flour

Beat egg whites until stiff, then add sugar on low speed. Fold in lightly beaten egg yolks and then remaining ingredients. Pour into cake tin and bake. Mix topping ingredients until smooth and pour onto hot cake. As the cake cools, the icing will set.

Auntie Mary's Passover Nut Cake

POLAND   Irene Gee

Preparation 10 mins   **Gas No 4, 350°F, 185°C**   **Cook 40 mins approx**   **Advance**

8 oz ground walnuts or hazelnuts (225 g)   2 tsp cocoa powder
8 oz caster sugar (225 g)   6 eggs, separated

Beat the egg whites until stiff. Beat the yolks and sugar until they are creamy. Fold in the nuts and cocoa and then fold the mixture into the egg whites. Bake in well-greased and lined 8″ (20 cm) loose-bottomed tin until a skewer comes out clean.

Tante Hedda's Nusstorte

AUSTRIA   Suzy Landes

Serves 8–10 Preparation 10 mins Gas No 6, 400°F, 200°C Cook 45 mins Advance
Freezable

9 oz ground hazelnuts (250 g)   8 oz sugar (225 g)
Juice and rind of 1 orange   7 eggs, separated

Blend sugar and egg yolks, add orange juice and rind and ground hazelnuts. Whisk the egg whites in a separate bowl. Fold the egg whites into the hazelnut mixture. Bake in a greased 10″ (25 cm) spring-form tin for approximately 45 minutes until cooked.

Apfelsinentorte – Orange Cake

GERMANY

Mrs H. Kochmann

Preparation 15 mins   **Gas No 5, 375°F, 190°C**   **Cook 30 mins**   **Advance**

Cake
6 eggs, separated
4½ oz caster sugar (125 g)
8¾ oz ground almonds (250 g)
1 orange

Icing
Grated rind and juice of ½ orange
6 oz icing sugar (170 g)
Decoration
6 orange slices

9½" spring-form cake tin (24 cm)

Beat egg yolks and sugar until creamy and the mixture holds the trail of the beaters. Gradually add orange juice and rind, then fold in ground almonds and finally the stiffly beaten egg whites. Bake for barely 30 minutes.
Icing: Mix icing ingredients together and spoon over top of cooled cake. Decorate with slices of orange.

Palachinken Torte – Pancake Cake

AUSTRIA/HUNGARY

Marta Gross

Preparation 15 mins   **Gas No 4, 350°F, 185°C**   **Cook 15 mins approx**

Ingredients
20 pancakes
1 jar apricot jam (preferably Hungarian)
4–6 oz ground walnuts (115–170 g)
2 oz granulated sugar (55 g)
½ tsp cinnamon

Topping
2–3 egg whites
1 tbls sugar
1 tbls ground walnuts

1 spring-form cake tin, greased

Mix granulated sugar with ground walnuts and cinnamon. Line the bottom of the cake tin with 2 pancakes and sprinkle liberally with walnut mixture. Place a pancake on top and spread with apricot jam. Repeat this process, alternating a layer of walnut and sugar mixture with one of apricot jam, until all pancakes are used. This part of the cake may be prepared several hours in advance.
Topping: Beat egg whites with sugar and walnuts until stiff. Pile on top of pancakes and place in oven. When cooked, carefully remove ring, leaving cake on base. Serve warm, cut into wedges.
Optional extra: A small jug of chocolate sauce may be served with the pancake cake.

Pischinger Torte

CZECHOSLOVAKIA   Mariette Demuth

Preparation 15 mins   **Advance**

1 packet Oblaten (round wafers)   5 oz icing sugar (140 g)
5 oz chocolate (140 g)   5 oz unsalted butter (140 g)
6 tsps milk   1 egg yolk

Mix the icing sugar, butter, chocolate and milk over a low heat – do not boil. When dissolved, remove from heat and add egg yolk. Spread while still hot over each wafer and build up in layers. Cover sides with any remaining mixture. Allow to cool.

Plum Cake for Chanukah

ENGLAND

Preparation 20 mins   **Gas No 2, 300°F, 160°C**   **Cook 3½ hrs**   **Advance**

6 oz butter (170 g)   ¼ tsp bicarbonate of soda
3 eggs   8 oz sultanas (225 g)
4 oz candied peel, sliced thinly (115 g)   8 oz currants (225 g)
1 tbls treacle or golden syrup   8 oz flour (225 g)
6 oz brown sugar (170 g)   A little mixed spice
2 oz almonds, blanched and chopped (55 g)
¼ pint hot milk (140 ml)   8" round cake tin (20 cm)

Line the cake tin with 3 thicknesses of greaseproof paper, letting the paper come 2" (5 cm) above the top of the tin. Warm the butter slightly and cream it with the sugar. Add the eggs, one at a time, and then beat in the treacle. Mix in the fruit, nuts and peel, then the flour and mixed spice, and lastly the bicarbonate of soda dissolved in the milk. Mix all thoroughly and pour into cake tin. Bake. When quite cold, cover the cake with marzipan and then with royal icing.

Passover Pound Cake

ENGLAND

Joan Rosenberg

Preparation 10 mins   **Gas No 3, 325°F, 180°C**   **Cook 1 hr**

4 large eggs
8½ oz caster sugar (240 g)
13 tbls oil
4½ oz potato flour (125 g)
4½ oz ground almonds (125 g)
1 tsp baking powder

2 tbls vanilla sugar
Flaked almonds

9″ × 9″ (23 × 23 cm) cake tin, greased
    and dusted with fine matzo meal

Separate 3 of the eggs and beat the whites until peaked. Add 4 oz (115 g) sugar and beat again. Beat 1 whole egg and the egg yolk with the remainder of the sugar until creamy. Beat in oil and then add all the dry ingredients except flaked almonds. Lastly fold in egg whites. Place mixture in tin and sprinkle with flaked almonds. Bake in the middle of the oven.

Variations: A marble cake can be made by mixing a quarter of the recipe with a tablespoon cocoa powder. Put spoonfuls of basic mixture and chocolate mixture into tin. Another variation is to use grated chocolate or chocolate vermicelli instead of cocoa powder.

Raspberry and Cinnamon Torte

AUSTRIA

Gladys Levy

Preparation 15 mins   Gas No 4, 350°F, 185°C   Cook 45 mins   Advance   Freezable

Cake
5 oz soft margarine (145 g)
1 egg
5 oz caster sugar (145 g)
1 tsp cinnamon
5 oz ground almonds (145 g)
8 oz raspberries (225 g)
5 oz S.R. flour (145 g)

Sauce (optional)
8 oz raspberries (225 g)
1 tbls lemon juice
1 tbls icing sugar
Thick yoghurt (optional)
To decorate
Ground cinnamon and icing sugar

8″ spring-form cake tin, greased and base-
    lined with greaseproof paper (20 cm)

Preheat oven. Place margarine, caster sugar, ground almonds, flour, egg and cinnamon in food processor and process. Spread half the mixture in tin and flatten lightly with fork. Sprinkle with raspberries and dot with remaining mixture so that it almost covers the fruit. Stand tin on a baking sheet and bake for 45 minutes. Cover with foil if becoming too brown. Cool in tin for 1 hour.

To serve: Turn out cake and dust with mixture of cinnamon and icing sugar. Serve cake warm with a sauce if desired. To make the sauce, purée the raspberries and then stir in icing sugar and lemon juice. If desired, add 1 tablespoon of thick yoghurt to the sauce.

Strudel

RUSSIA   Frances Ravden

Preparation 10 mins   Gas No 6, 400°F, 200°C   Cook 30 mins   Advance   Freezable

Pastry
1 lb plain flour (450 g)
2 eggs
3 dsp oil
3 dsp caster sugar

Filling
Jam
1 cup sultanas
Cinnamon
1 tbls sugar
Breadcrumbs

Mix pastry ingredients together to make a soft dough. Roll out very thinly into a large rectangle. Brush with a thin layer of oil, then spread with a thin layer of jam and sprinkle over some breadcrumbs, sultanas, sugar and cinnamon. Moisten edges so they will stick together and gently roll up the pastry. Grease a flat tin with oil, place the roll on it and brush top with a little oil. Bake in a hot oven.

Walnut Cake

ENGLAND

Preparation 15 mins   Gas No 4, 350°F, 185°C   Cook 45 mins   Advance

Cake
6 oz breadcrumbs, soaked in rum (170 g)
6 oz shelled walnuts (170 g)
10 oz caster sugar (285 g)
6 eggs, separated

Icing
10 oz icing sugar, sieved (285 g)
Juice of half a lemon
6 drops hot water

Beat yolks and caster sugar together, add pounded walnuts and breadcrumbs and fold in stiffly beaten egg whites. Turn into a well greased cake tin and bake. Allow to cool. *Icing*: Put icing sugar in a small basin and place this in a large bowl containing hot water. Add lemon juice and water. Stir quickly and spread over the cake at once. Decorate with pieces of walnut. (Substitute matzo meal for the breadcrumbs at Pesach.)

Orah Torte – Walnut Cake

YUGOSLAVIA   Bulka Danon

Preparation 30 mins   **Gas No 6, 400°F, 200°C**   **Cook 1 hr**   **Advance**

Cake   *Filling*
8 eggs, separated   2 oz chocolate (55 g)
8 tbls walnuts, chopped   2 tbls water
8 tbls caster sugar   1 egg yolk
8 tbls breadcrumbs   1 tbls sugar
8 tbls water   8 oz butter (225 g)
                                                   Juice of 1 lemon
Two 10″ cake tins (25 cm)   1 tsp coffee powder

Cake: Beat egg yolks with all cake ingredients except the egg whites for 5 minutes. Beat egg whites until stiff and fold into yolk mixture. Pour into cake tins and cook on Gas No 6, 400°F, 200°C for 30 minutes then lower the temperature to Gas No 3, 325°F, 180°C for another 30 minutes. Allow to cool.

Filling: Heat chocolate and water until chocolate has melted. Beat egg yolk with sugar and add to the chocolate. Beat in the butter, lemon juice and coffee until smooth. Allow to cool. Use to sandwich the cakes.

MISCELLANEOUS

Preserves

Eingemacht I – Beetroot Jam

RUSSIA   Barbara Tobias

Preparation 20 mins   **Cook 2½ hrs**

2 lb beetroot, peeled (900 g)   **2 lb sugar (900 g)**
2 lemons   **Ginger to taste**
Handful of blanched almonds   **2 glasses cold water**

After washing well, cut beetroot into small pieces. Put with sugar into saucepan over a low heat and stir until sugar dissolves. Add juice of lemons and boil for 2½ hours. Add almonds and ginger. Remove from heat and add 2 glasses of cold water. Stir.
Alternative method using a microwave oven (for an 800 watt oven):
Grate beetroot and place in a large microwave bowl with the sugar. Do not cover. Cook on high power for 10 minutes, stirring occasionally with a wooden spoon until sugar has melted. Add juice of lemons and cook again on high power for approximately 20 minutes, stirring occasionally. Test for setting towards the end, and take care not to burn mixture. Add ginger and nuts and cook on high power for 2 minutes. Remove from oven, add 2 glasses of cold water and stir.
After mixture is cooked (using either method), leave to cool slightly. Stir and then pot in sterilized jars and seal.

This jam is traditionally served at Pesach.

Eingemacht II – Beetroot Jam

LATVIA   Elinor Corfan

Preparation 10 mins   **Cook 1½ hrs**

4 lb beetroot (1.8 kg)   3 lb sugar (1.35 kg)
2 tsp ground ginger   3 lemons, rind and juice
4 oz almonds, coarsely chopped (115 g)

Peel beetroots and cut into strips like matches. Put in a pan, cover with water and cook gently until tender. Then add sugar, grated rind and juice of lemons and ginger and stir until sugar has dissolved. Bring to the boil and cook gently until mixture is thick and clear – about 1 hour. Add almonds a few minutes before removing pan from the heat. Pour mixture into warm jars and seal. Jam should have a slightly crunchy texture.

Traditionally served at Pesach.

Sweetmeats

Apricot Pletzlach

SOUTH AFRICA   Rebecca Symons

Preparation 15 mins   **Soaking time overnight**   **Cook 30 mins**

2 lb 2 oz dried apricots (1 kg)   2 oranges, peeled
8 cups sugar   1 cup boiling water for soaking

Soak apricots overnight in a cupful of boiling water. Remove all loose pith from oranges and discard and mince orange flesh together with the apricots. Place fruit mixture in a pan and add the sugar. Boil for 25 minutes, stirring all the time, until a little dropped into a saucer of water sets. Heat must be fairly high. Pour onto a wet pastry board, smooth with a wooden spoon and when cold cut into squares or diamonds with a non-serrated knife.

Stuffed Dates

PORTUGAL & GIBRALTAR   Judy Jackson

Preparation 20 mins   **Cook 15 mins approx**

5 oz ground almonds (140 g)   *Caramel*
2 oz caster sugar (55 g)   4 oz granulated sugar (115 g)
3 fl oz water (90 ml)   6 fl oz water (180 ml)
1 box preserved dates   1 dsp liquid glucose

Make a syrup with the sugar and water, bring to the boil and keep on the heat for about 2 minutes. Add syrup to the ground almonds to make a paste. Stone each date and fill with a small rolled piece of almond paste. To make the caramel, bring sugar, water and glucose to the boil, stirring only once or twice. Continue boiling until the syrup reaches the crack stage (about 280°F, 140°C). To test, drizzle a little syrup into cold water – if it forms needles which snap, the syrup is ready. Remove pan from heat, drop dates in one at a time, take out and place on an oiled surface. Leave until quite cold. Wipe bases to remove any oil and place in paper cases.

These are traditional Sephardi sweets which are eaten at Purim.

Halwa

INDIA

Preparation 10 mins   **Cook 30 mins**

12 oz jaggery (coarse dark brown sugar)   2 oz wheat flour (55 g)
    (320 g)   2 oz fresh coconut, grated (55 g)
4 oz rice flour (115 g)   ¼ tsp saffron
¼ pint water (150 ml)   1 tbls poppy seeds
1 tbls ground cardamom   2 tbls sliced almonds or pistachios

Melt jaggery in a non-stick pan, then gradually add rice flour, wheat flour, coconut and water, stirring mixture constantly. Cook for 20 minutes, stirring occasionally. When mixture begins to thicken and leave the sides of the pan, add cardamom and saffron. Place a teaspoonful of the mixture on a plate to see if it will set. When it is ready, pour mixture on to a greased plate and smooth. Decorate with the nuts and seeds. When cool, cut into diamond shapes.

A traditional Chanukah dish which is also used by the Bene Israel Jews at Rosh Hashana.

Ingberlach

SOUTH AFRICA

Rebecca Symons

Preparation 5 mins

Cook 20–30 mins approx

1 lb grated carrots (450 g)
1 lb sugar (450 g)
1 dsp ginger

4 oz chopped almonds (115 g)
Grated orange rind, lemon juice (optional)

Boil sugar and carrots over a low heat, stirring frequently until mixture thickens (test by dropping a little into a saucer of water). Add ginger and almonds. Spread mixture onto a wet board, smooth with a wooden spoon and allow to set. When cold, cut into squares. Orange rind and/or lemon juice can be added with the ginger and almonds.

Orange Pletzlach

SOUTH AFRICA

Rebecca Symons

Preparation 10 mins

Cook 5–10 mins

6 navel oranges

Sugar

Boil whole oranges until soft (test with a fork). Remove from water and leave to cool. When cold, mince, then weigh. Add 1 pound of sugar for every pound of fruit. Put in a saucepan and simmer on a low heat, stirring frequently to prevent burning, until mixture leaves the sides of the pan. Pour onto a wet pastry board, smooth with a wooden spoon and when cold cut into squares or diamonds using a non-serrated knife.

Queijinhos

PORTUGAL   Judy Jackson

Makes 20   Preparation 20 mins   Cook 10–15 mins   Advance   Freezable

Cases
2 oz caster sugar (55 g)
3 fl oz water (85 ml)
5 oz ground almonds (140 g)

Jemma Filling
4 oz caster sugar (115 g)
2½ fl oz water (75 ml)
1 vanilla pod
6 egg yolks

Cases: Make a syrup with the sugar and water, bring to the boil and keep on the heat for approximately 2 minutes. Add syrup to the ground almonds and make a paste.

Filling: Put sugar, water and vanilla pod in a small pan. Bring to the boil, stirring once or twice until the sugar has melted. Once the syrup starts to boil do not stir but wash down the sides of the pan with a wet pastry brush. Continue boiling and brushing until the syrup makes a thread when tested between the thumb and first finger. At this stage, slowly pour syrup onto the beaten egg yolks. Return mixture to a double saucepan and stir until it thickens – do not let it boil. Then immediately stand the pan in cold water.

Make the almond paste into small balls, the size of a walnut, and make flat discs for the lids. Form each ball into a cup and fill each one with the cold jemma filling. Seal with a lid. Continue until all the almond paste is used up (this quantity makes about 20). The finished sweets should be about ¾" (2 cm) high and may be rolled in granulated sugar and stored in the refrigerator or freezer.

Served at Passover.

Drinks, Etc.

Hariri – Almond Milk

IRAQ

Preparation 10 mins

Cook 5 mins approx

3 cups water
1 cup almonds
5 tbls sugar

¼ tsp ground cardamom or 2 cardamom
pods

Grind almonds with water (use blender on high speed), then strain liquid through several layers of cheesecloth into a bowl, squeezing to extract all liquid. Add sugar and cardamom and cook over medium heat until liquid comes to the boil. Reduce heat and boil for one minute. The result will be quite a thick milk; dilute with boiling water for a thinner consistency.

This was traditionally used for breaking the fast on Yom Kippur.

Sour Milk/Cream

POLAND

Jane Finestone

Preparation 2 mins

Standing time 2 days

1 pint milk, not homogenised (½ litre)

Put milk in a large jar in a warm place for 2 days. The milk will thicken. Before serving in a summer soup, chill thoroughly. Can be served chilled with small new potatoes, chopped spring onions and a little chopped parsley.
Sour milk can also be turned into cheese by placing a jar containing the sour milk in a pan of hot water on a low heat. When the whey forms remove the pan and allow to cool. Tip the contents of the jar into a muslin cloth over a basin and allow it to drip all night. DO NOT SQUEEZE. To make richer, add a tablespoon of cream.
Sour milk was also beaten thoroughly and served in glasses with brown bread and butter.

Raisin Wine

ENGLAND   Janet Cohen

Preparation 5 mins   **Storage time 2 weeks minimum**

6 lb raisins (2.7 kg)   **8 pints water (4.5 litres)**
Sugar and cinnamon to taste

Place all ingredients in a large wine jar. Cover and leave.

This was traditionally served on Seder night.

Creamed Mushrooms Kolta

USA

Serves 8   **Preparation 15 mins**   **Cook 1 hr**   **Advance**

2 oz dried mushrooms (55 g)   **Salt**
1 lb button mushrooms, sliced (450 g)   **2 onions, minced**
2 tbls butter   **2 cups sour cream**
1 heaped tbls flour   **1 tbls lemon juice**
1 large egg

Wash the dried mushrooms, changing the water several times. Put in a pan, cover with water and add a pinch of salt. Bring to the boil, cover and simmer for 45 minutes. Remove the mushrooms from the cooking liquid and slice. Strain and reserve the liquid. Cover the fresh mushrooms with water in a pot. Bring to the boil, cover, and simmer for 10 minutes. Drain, reserving liquid, and add to the other mushrooms. Sauté onions in butter until golden. Combine flour, egg, sour cream and lemon juice with a whisk and then slowly heat this cream mixture, whisking constantly. Have half the mushroom broth in a pan and half in a bowl. Gradually add some of the broth from the bowl into the cream mixture, beating very hard with the whisk. Then pour this cream mixture into the broth in the pan, whisking constantly. Slowly heat this. Add any remaining broth, whisking hard. NEVER LET THIS MIXTURE BOIL. Pour over mushrooms and onion. Best served cold. Can be used as a sauce.

Split Peas

HUNGARY

Serves 10   **Preparation 5 mins**   **Cook 30 mins approx**   **Advance**

4¼ lb split peas (2 kg)   **Salt and ground black pepper**

Wash split peas thoroughly. Place in a saucepan and cover with water and cook until tender. Let the split peas cool and then add salt and pepper to taste.

This is traditionally served at circumcision ceremonies.

Merdumah – Spicy Relish

LIBYA

Eveleen Habib

Preparation 10 mins **Cook 1¼ hrs approx** **Advance**

2 lb tomatoes, skinned (900 g)
3–4 cloves of garlic, chopped
Salt and black pepper

1 chilli pepper, chopped and deseeded
3 tbls olive oil

Place all ingredients in a saucepan and bring to the boil on a medium heat. Leave to simmer until the liquid has evaporated. Stir occasionally.

This can be eaten as an accompaniment to any meat, or with bread. We also put it in a frying pan, without oil, and break 2 eggs over it and cook gently. Another option is to cut up spicy sausages and cook them in this sauce with the eggs. (In Libya this is known as Shakshuka, though in other North African countries this dish is made differently.)

INDEX

WEIGHTS AND MEASURES

Whilst every effort has been made to ensure that the recipes conform to Jewish dietary laws, we have had to leave it to you, the cook, to check on the Kashrut of some individual ingredients, e.g. wine, cheese, wine vinegar, gelatine, etc.

DRY MEASURE			LIQUID MEASURE		
	1 oz	28 grms	1	tablespoon	1	tablespoon
	2 oz	56 grms	2	tablespoons	2	tablespoons
	3 oz	85 grms	3	tablespoons	3	tablespoons
	3½ oz	100 grms	4	tablespoons	4	tablespoons
(¼ lb)	4 oz	114 grms	5	tablespoons	1	decilitre
	5 oz	142 grms	6	tablespoons	1¼	decilitres
	6 oz	170 grms	8	tablespoons (¼ pint)	1½	decilitres
	7 oz	198 grms	¼	pint – generous	2	decilitres
(½ lb)	8 oz	225 grms	½	pint – scant	¼	litre (2½ DL)
(¼ kilo)	8¾ oz	250 grms	½	pint	3	decilitres
	9 oz	256 grms	¾	pint	½	litre – scant
	10 oz	283 grms	¾	pint – generous	½	litre
	11 oz	312 grms	1	pint	½	litre – generous
	12 oz	340 grms	1¼	pints	¾	litre
	13 oz	368 grms	1½	pints	1	litre – scant
	14 oz	400 grms	1¾	pints	1	litre
	15 oz	425 grms	2	pints	1	litre – generous
(1 lb)	16 oz	450 grms	2½	pints	1¼	litres
(½ kilo)	17½ oz	500 grms	3	pints	1½	litres
	1½ lbs	700 grms	3½	pints	2	litres
			4	pints	2¼	litres
			4½	pints	2½	litres
			5	pints	3	litres

OVEN TEMPERATURE GUIDE

Gas No.	Fahrenheit	Centigrade	Description
¼	225	120	
½	250	140	Very Cool
1	275	150	
2	300	160	Cool or Slow
3	325	180	
4	350	185	Moderate
5	375	190	
6	400	200	Moderately Hot
7	425	220	
8	450	230	Hot
9	475	240	Very Hot

2 level tablespoons of flour = 1 oz
A British pint = 20 fl ozs
A British cup = 10 fl ozs

1 level tablespoon of sugar = 1 oz
An American pint = 16 fl ozs
An American cup = 8 fl ozs